Can *Art* Save Us?

by
Fred Mandell

The photos in this book are printed in black & white.

To view them in color, simply scan the QR code below using your smart phone or tablet. The images are shown online in the order they appear in the book.

You can also view them online at:
www.fredmandell.com/canartsaveus

Foreword
by
Nancy J. Adler

Leadership Artistry

*Only by investing in the artistry of our humanity
will we create a peaceful, prosperous planet*

"These times are riven with anxiety and uncertainty" asserts poet, philosopher, and management consultant John O'Donohue.[1] "In the hearts of people some natural ease has been broken. …Our trust in the future has lost its innocence. We know now that anything can happen. … The traditional structures of shelter are shaking, their foundations revealed to be no longer stone but sand. We are suddenly thrown back on ourselves. Politics, religion and economics, and the institutions of family and community, all have become abruptly unsure. At first, it sounds completely naive to suggest that now might be the time to invoke beauty. Yet this is exactly what … [we claim]. Why? Because there is nowhere else to turn and we are desperate; furthermore, it is because we have so disastrously neglected the Beautiful that we now find ourselves in such a terrible crisis."[2]

Twenty-first century society yearns for a leadership of possibility, a leadership based more on hope, aspiration, innovation, and beauty than on the replication of historical patterns of constrained pragmatism. Luckily, such a leadership is possible today. For the first time in history, leaders can work backward from their aspirations and imagination rather than forward from the past.[3] "The gap between what people

i

can imagine and what they can accomplish has never been smaller."[4]

Responding to the challenges and yearnings of the twenty-first century demands the practices and perspectives of artists. Designing options worthy of implementation calls for levels of inspiration, creativity, and a passionate commitment to beauty that, until recently, have been more the province of artists and artistic processes than the domain of most managers.[5] The time is right for the artistic imagination of each of us to co-create the leadership that the world most needs and deserves.

The Talmud, among many ancient traditions, reminds us that "We don't see things as they are; we see things as we are." Fred Mandell, with his unique fusion of executive experience, artistic creativity, and profound humanity presents the world as only he can see it. Through an equally singular blending of memoir, storytelling, poetry and reflections on the creative process, Fred challenges us to believe in the power of art and art-making to transform the maker, the viewer and the broader community. He calls upon us to introduce the aspiration for beauty into conversations at all levels of society. *Can Art Save Us?*, offers a rare and precious opportunity to see the world, not as it is, but as it could be; not as we habitually see it –reinforced daily by yet another onslaught of the horrifying, sensationalized cacophony masquerading as the morning news –but as we yearn to see it and to live in it. That yearning is not for some idealized utopia, but for a world that grants us efficacy – the efficacy of our reclaimed belief in 'Yes': Yes we can make the world (and our country, community, and organizations) better. We yearn for a world that reflects our collective humanity, and the belief that "Yes, we can achieve it."

Philosopher and scholar Thomas Kuhn, in explaining how thought systems change, counsels that it is impossible to see something new until you have a metaphor that will let you perceive it in new ways.[6] So to be able to invent a new, more peaceful, prosperous, sustainable, and beautiful world, each of us needs first to change ourselves and our own thinking. To be able to change our thinking, we must first change the metaphors through which we view the world. In asking the question "Can art save us?", Fred offers us just such a new metaphor. Not surprisingly, in the process of opening to this new metaphor and new way of thinking, we find ourselves unfolding to the possibility of beauty.

What allows individuals, organizations, and whole societies to let go of prior worldviews and approaches that seemingly worked in the past but are no longer either appropriate or efficacious? To even ask the right questions requires profound courage and commitment. Otherwise, the completely human response would be resignation - "Why bother?" Canadian Ian Wilson wisely observed that "No amount of sophistication is going to allay the fact that all your knowledge is about the past and all your decisions are about the future."[7] To move ahead in spite of not knowing, which is where profound hope and commitment lead people, is to embrace the unknown, while not yet knowing if it will ultimately become knowable or continue to remain beyond the grasp of our understanding. Art offers us, artists and non-artists alike, pathways into just such commitments and courage. As Fred reveals in *Can Art Save Us?* artistic processes offer

iii

us a way to face unacceptable reality, to confront the unknown and unknowable, to marry aspiration with empiricism, and ultimately to expose leadership as the embodiment of artistic processes, and not merely the application of ever more sophisticated analytical algorithms. As Roger Martin, former Dean of Toronto's Rotman School of Management wisely observed, "What the world needs is more business artists, not more business analysts." *Can Art Save Us?* invites us to bring the studio out into the world and to begin reclaiming our capacities as leadership artists. Ultimately, Fred's work is a tribute to what we are individually and collectively capable of, unfettered by a regrettable past or a daunting present. In the words of singer/songwriter Phil Ochs:

"In these ugly times,
the only true protest is beauty."

---

[1] O'Donohue, J. (2003:2). *Beauty: The invisible embrace.* NY: Harper Perennial

[2] Op cit, 2-3; also see Adler, N.J. (2015, in press) "Global Wisdom: Not a Panacea, but absolutely Necessary for Transcending Yesterday's Managerial Failures" in Anders Ortenblad (ed.), *Handbook of Research on Management Ideas and Panaceas: Adaptation and Context.* Cheltenham, U.K. & Northampton, MA: Edward Elgar.

[3] Paragraph based on Adler, N. J. (2006). The arts and leadership: Now that we can do anything, what will we do? *Academy of Management Learning and Education,* 5(4), 466-499.

[4] Hamel, G. (2000:10). *Leading the revolution.* Boston, Mass.: Harvard Business School Press

[5] See Adler, N.J. (2011) "Leading Beautifully: The Creative Economy and Beyond", *Journal of Management Inquiry*, vol. 20 (no. 3), pp. 208-221.

[6] Kuhn, T.(1962) *The Structure of Scientific Revolutions.* Chicago: The University of Chicago Press.

[7] Wilson as cited at: http://home.bi.no/fgl88001/sigs.htm

Life is not what one lived
but what one remembers
and how one remembers it
in order to recount it.
       -Gabriel Garcia Marquez

The purpose of art is to lay
bare the questions that have
been hidden by the answers.
       -James Baldwin

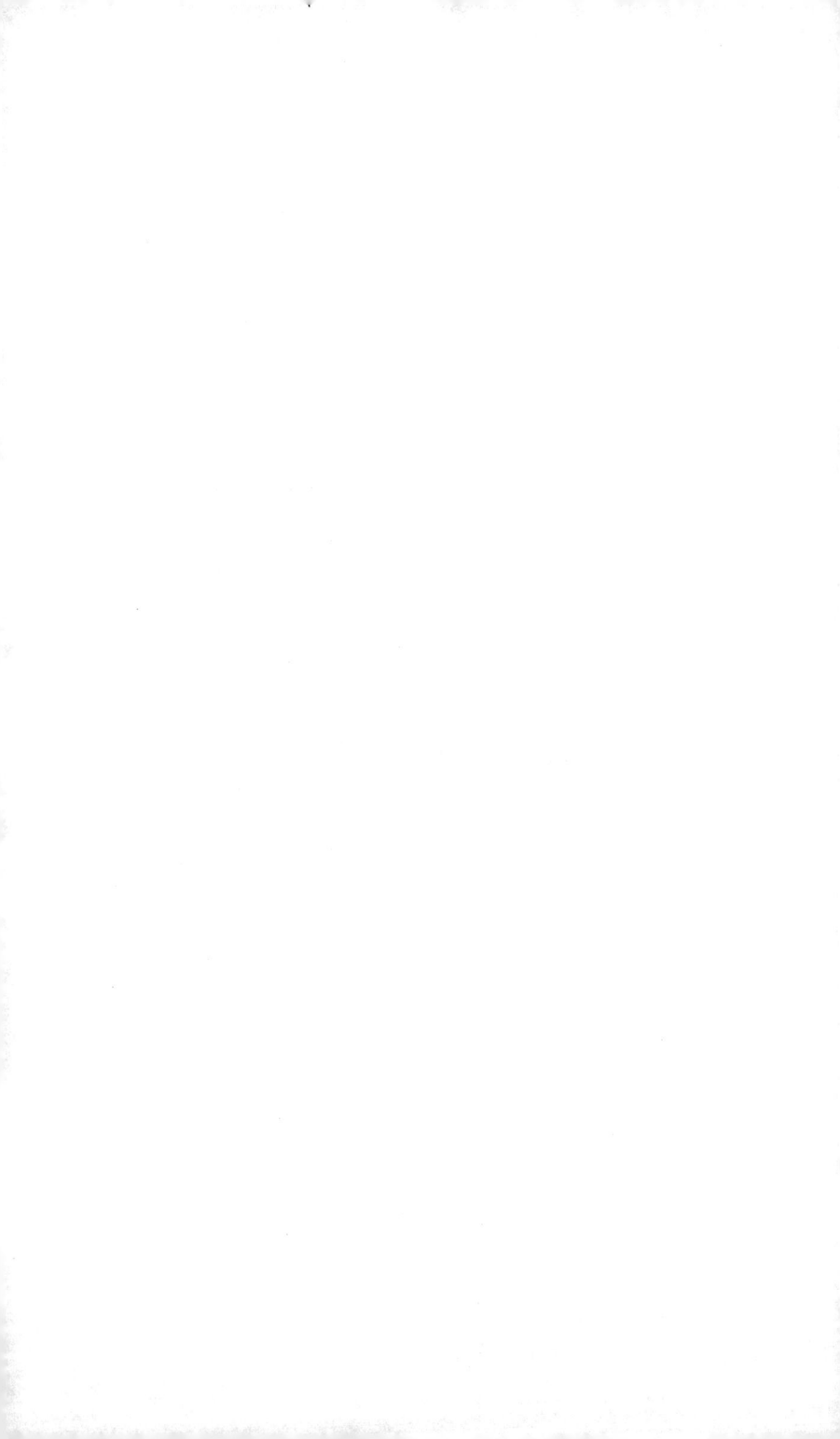

Introduction

Picasso once observed tongue in cheek that he begins with an idea and then it becomes something else. I don't think that is unique to Picasso. Anyone who has engaged in a creative project has experienced this phenomenon. In fact, that seems to be a good description of life itself. We begin with an idea of ourselves and then it becomes something else.

Beginning with an idea and becoming something else perfectly describes the journey of *Can Art Save Us?*

Over a two year period I worked on a series of five paintings which I came to entitle *Memory Calls*. The paintings were an effort to recapture and preserve the people and events in the first five years of my life.

While working on the series, I began to record reflections on the experience in my sketchbook. Sometimes these recordings took the form of idea bursts that unpredictably exploded in my head while painting, such as "Nothing Protected, Everything Open." Sometimes they formed into longer reflections. I soon discovered an interesting interplay between the painting and the writing. Painting brought me deeper into the writing. And writing brought me deeper into the painting. This was the organic process that has led to this book. In fact, *Can Art Save Us?* is the "something else" that started with the painting series *Memory Calls*. I had no idea when I began the paintings that they would lead to a book! Or that the outcome would be so transformative.

Painting and writing are different processes. There are also many points of intersection. I suppose this is true of many kinds of creative endeavor. For me, creative endeavor comes in the widest array of forms. We naturally think of the traditional forms when we throw out the word creativity such as painting, poetry, music, dance, theater, crafts. But for me it also includes virtually every form of human endeavor which, in their underlying elements, are creative, whether we are talking about creating relationships, creating enterprises, creating teams, creating a home life or creating who we are. None of these endeavors is passive and all require the same dynamic elements and skills as are necessary in the more traditionally defined creative fields.

For those who think this book is exclusively for artists I would offer this additional invitation to read on. If we are not all artists, most of us are appreciators of one form of art or another. Perhaps we enjoy a good concert or crafts show or dramatic performance live on stage or on TV. We all consume art in some fashion or another. What is essential is that beyond the experience of consuming art we have an opportunity to learn from the actual process of making that which we consume.

Art is both experience and process. And what comes out of a mindful and purposeful engagement with art is a deeper level of personal insight and growth and a broader appreciation of the possibilities in our world.

Over the past 25 years there has been a great deal of research about creativity and the brain. We have moved beyond an initial view that the left side of the brain houses our analytic capabilities while the right side taps into our intuition and imagination. Today we generally believe that creative capacity emerges from an integrated set of brain functions often referred to as a "whole brain" capability. It is this fully integrated whole brain consciousness—I call it an art mindset—that I believe not only engages creativity but builds self efficacy and is critical if we are going to survive and thrive in the 21st century.

Can Art Save Us? is shaped by three broad questions:

- Where do ideas come from?
- What happens to ideas in the process of making them come alive?
- Does the process taking place within the studio have relevance to the wider world, in other words, can the art-making process offer insights, frameworks and capabilities that can make a difference in dealing with the challenging world we currently inhabit?

Before we get to this last question we travel through the actual process of creating the five paintings that make up *Memory Calls.* At the heart of the paintings is the role of memory in our lives and the notion that memory itself is a form of creative expression. The task of giving voice (in my case, imagery and words) to our memories is not an easy one, since memory by its nature is random, episodic and often disjointed. Yet one of the things we seek through creative expression is meaning and narrative coherence. How do we deal with this fundamental paradox? Without revealing how I chose to respond, let's simply say that without this paradox the quest would not be a creative one. It would simply be a recapitulation. It is precisely because of this tension between our crazy quilt memories and the search for meaning and coherence that we are driven to give expression to something new that comes out of the struggle. In other words, we are ourselves living paradoxes. One way I have confronted this dilemma is to weave into the account of creating the paintings the actual memories that inspired them. In this sense I have tried to have the book reflect many of the characteristics of memory itself.

I also found that in the process of writing *Can Art Save Us?* I could not resist extending my reflections to the wider world beyond the studio walls. Here's one place where the something else inserted itself. For some this may appear to be a stretch and a dangerous diversion from a commonly held view regarding the boundaries between art, creativity and the harsh, tough minded world beyond the studio. In other words, art should know its place and artists should leave reality to those who can stand the heat. There will be some (and I certainly respect this point of view) who will say the artist must focus on his art and fully develop himself with full concentration and not be distracted by the machinations of a troubled world. I wrestled with this separation at length. And in the end I could not abide it. I have come to a different perspective. So I gave into my impulses and allowed my reflections to spill over into the wider world under the basic notion that artists are also citizens of the world. I am not claiming that every artist should become a social activist. There are lots of colors in the rainbow of art and creativity. I am rather saying that art as a framework and process has something meaningful to contribute to the way we look at the world and how we solve the world's problems. In fact, I would go so far as to say that a world that does not embrace art and the art making endeavor as central to its way of being is in great danger of not only limiting our options but also of diminishing the human spirit. And then this process of reflection brought me all the way to the view that art, rather than being a separate and perhaps rarefied undertaking, is in fact a form of engagement that can transform the world.

So it might surprise the reader to find him/herself reading reflections toward the last quarter of the book on the state of the world, leadership and the relationship between art and its relevance beyond the studio walls. For me this trajectory has been natural and even obvious. I cannot explain whether this is a reflection of my personal sensibilities or whether the content of the paintings catapulted me onto this trajectory. The American Abstract Expressionist painter Jackson Pollock said: "Every good painter paints what he is." As the reader will discover I am Grandpas Meyer and Harry, Grandmas Sarah and Dora, my aunts and uncles and mother and father and Brooklyn and the promise of Long Island inferred but never fulfilled. I wonder about unfinished lives. And secrets and the petty crimes of a five year old, the shames of which have remained in the substrata of his being. All the memories of these relationships and places prompted questions that would not let go of me. What was the meaning of their lives? What are their voices continuing to whisper to me? For me, living with and remembering the events and experiences of the first five years of my life and trying to express a kind of cohesion out of these often disconnected memories led me to reflect on the nature of our responsibility to those memories. For me, it was an easy next step into the state of our current world and the dangers we face. I believe we are in an economic, environmental and spiritual crisis. And yet I hold out hope because underlying the entire arch of this journey is what I believe is the transformational power of art. Art and imagination brought me to engage with memory.

And it is art and imagination that I believe, have the power to mend the world.

Others may find it a bit of a leap to bridge from a series of paintings about memory to a clarion call for leaders to embrace art. There may be those who hold to the idea that art and leadership are two very distinctive things. And the wall of skepticism that separates them is there for good reason. I would, however, beg to strongly differ. I can only say, read on. Perhaps the journey of reading this book will take the reader someplace s/he has not been before. I hope that by the end of the book the reader will not only see the connection, but feel it in the gut.

I came to this point in my own journey through some perhaps odd twists.

My formal training was as an academic, having earned a doctorate in history from the University of Chicago. But I quickly learned I did not enjoy research or scholarship so I bounced around for a few years. I wrote a novel, got involved with a consulting group engaged in social change in mid-sized cities and dabbled in real estate. In other words, I was a bit lost. Then one very clear spring day I came very close to being killed in a car accident which landed me in the hospital for an extended stay followed by several months of recuperation. My son Jacob was almost 4 and my wife Karen was pregnant with our daughter Hinda at the time of the accident. My motivations turned toward supporting my family so I found myself knocking on the door of a financial services company that ultimately became American Express Financial Advisors. That knock turned into a 21 year career with the company that led to increasing levels of responsibility and titles. I built the company's number one sales division. During this period, the notion of the "corporate athlete" had been floating around—that is someone within an organization who did not necessarily have deep specialized expertise but had the versatility to move about an organization and take on diverse leadership roles. I was tapped to be one such "corporate athlete." I became the Chief Operating Officer of an investment company which we grew to $3.5 billion under management and consecutive years of record earnings. This led to an opportunity to lead multiple marketing businesses for the company. And toward the end of my stay I got involved in developing a global strategy for delivering financial advice including the evaluation of potential mergers and acquisitions.

But in my early 50's I felt some grumblings inside me. I had no idea what they were, only that I needed to pay attention to them. On a whim I enrolled in a sculpture workshop. I had not taken an art class since the seventh grade but I quickly became hooked on every aspect of creating bronze sculptures. Under the tutelage of wonderfully talented and patient teachers, I slowly began to learn the many sub-crafts that went into creating a sculpture. After three years my teachers told me I was ready to have my own one person show and when folks began plunking down good hard cash for my pieces I didn't quite know what to make of it. At that point I decided to step away from the corporate world in order to pursue my interest in art. I did not envision myself becoming a full time artist. But I knew I had to travel further down the path of art to see where it led. So after 21 years with the company I stepped away.

Then one weekend when I was at the foundry for a bronze pour I got wacked by an insight. We were all dressed in our protective gear as we melted the small bronze ingots into an orange molten liquid. I could feel the heat as we raised the cauldron of molten bronze above the cement encased sculptures. As the liquid tipped over the tongue of the cauldron and began filling the crevices left empty from the melted wax, a thought hit me. The very process artists go through to create a body of work over a lifetime parallels the process leaders go through in creating a sustainable enterprise. Both involve a lot of heavy lifting, a lot of heat and a lot of craft, all informed by a larger vision and imagination.

That is when I first sensed the tremendous potential at the intersection of art and leadership.

Over the intervening years I have been working at that intersection, in some instances, bringing programs and workshops into organizations. In others, bringing leaders through an immersive program called The Leader's Studio. I have taught programs at MIT Sloan School of Management to MBA students and Advanced Fellows under the title "The Leader as Artist" and I have spoken at Executive Education programs. I also began to shift my focus from sculpture to painting and drawing. I felt at a certain point that in order to grow as an artist I needed to learn the basic language of the visual arts—drawing—and to play with the flat surface of a canvas. For the past 9 years I have been concentrating on painting.

As I have continued to reflect, write, teach and work directly with organizational leaders my thinking has evolved from a focus on delivering content and programs to a much broader and strategic sense of the need to insert art and the language of beauty into the leadership conversation. And so still another shift has occurred. With an amazing group of artists, academics and entrepreneurs, community leaders I recently launched The Global Institute for the Arts and Leadership

8

(www.artschangeleaders.org). Our mission is to create a more peaceful, sustainable and beautiful world by developing transformational leaders worldwide through the arts. In many ways, The Global Institute for the Arts and Leadership is my response to the question posed in the book's title: *Can Art Save Us?* In truth, I don't have a definitive answer to my own question. But it will not be for the lack of trying.

Can Art Save Us? is not a conventional book with chapters. These pages are rather a verbal collage—reflections, anecdotes, stories, memoir, poems, koans, visual images—which I hope have the cumulative effect of taking the reader on a journey down one path, perhaps never taken before, then another and another until together we come to the end—of the book at least—looking at ourselves and the world differently.

If, as I argue here, art and the language of beauty has an indispensable role to play in our wider world then there is much more work to be done. While *Can Art Save Us?* begins as a deeply personal book, it is perhaps also the first brush stroke on a broader canvas.

Can *Art* Save Us?

Is dedicated to my family - past, present and future

Karen, Jacob, Julie, Baylor, Cameron, Hinda, Matt, Mirabelle, Becky, Doug, Hannah Rose, Judy, Dan, Ben, Jed, Mimsi, Susie, Mary, Richard, Julie, Abby, Matt, Nina, Irving (Mandy), Helen, Martin, Rose, Harry, Sarah, Meyer and Dora.

To see is to forget the name of the thing one sees.
-Paul Valery

As is often the case in life I have arrived at this unexpected place unexpectedly.

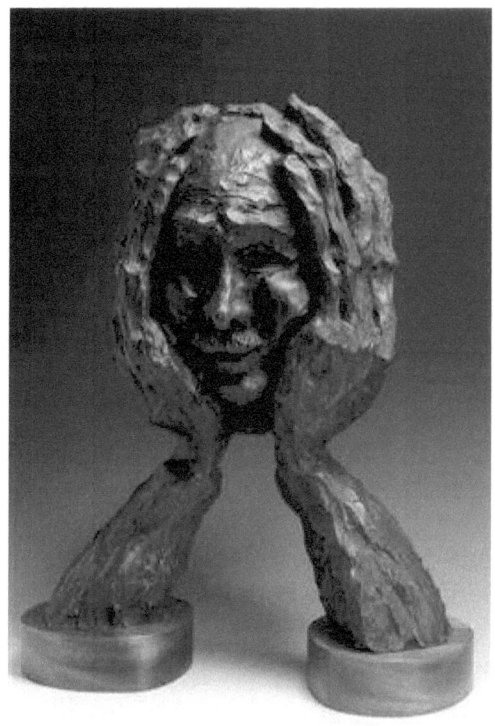

Bronze Self Portrait

I believe this is the nature of creativeness:

It is filled with surprise and wonder. It is filled with risk and fear, sometimes with despair, sometimes with exhilaration. Creativeness is that continuous state of creativity during which we are connected to something that has no name and we are ripe with aliveness. And

15

always with paradox. These pages started as an effort at self understanding, an effort to explore how a series of paintings called *Memory Calls* came into being and what happened throughout the process of creating.

I began with three basic questions.

Where do ideas come from?

What happens during the process of making ideas come alive?

Does any of this have relevance beyond the studio walls—in the wider world?

Of course the questions can go on and on, each one raising another.

And then these reflections became something else—a journey of being both lost and found.

The Natural Order of Things

How is it possible to be both lost and found at the same time? Many of us live lives of seeking—we read books, we experiment, we take courses, we go on retreats, we go down one path—and then another, and then a different path. But we never seem to find the ultimate answer, the one we are seeking to fully embrace, the true path, a calling and we wonder what is wrong with us. I do not believe there is anything wrong with us. We are both lost and found.

We live in paradox and that is the natural order of things. Paradox is the source of confusion and the portal to creative energy. It is where we wrestle with perplexity and stumble across insight.

Holding Opposing Ideas

These thoughts about paradox came to me during a talk I gave at an Innovation Summit. I offered to the audience the notion that when I was painting I was both lost and found. I was lost because from a creative perspective I did not know what came next. Worse, I did not know how to get from here to there. In many respects I was a novice, an apprentice. Frustration ran high. My mood darkened. I felt like a failure. I tried one thing after another. I painted on stretched canvas. I tore and hung canvas from a roll and tacked it to the wall. I scraped and painted over. I tried spontaneous action painting with wild, angry strokes and more deliberate, thoughtful strokes. I could not break through. I realized it was not a matter of technique that blocked my progress. I wanted to throw all these markings in the garbage. I was lost. But then I walked away. I stood back. I followed da Vinci's advice—"to go away, go some distance away"—and I realized I was found because I was on the path I was meant to be on. As frustrated as I felt, as bereft of hope as I felt, I knew I had to continue. I was where I belonged. I was both lost and found.

After the talk a woman came up to me and asked, how do you live through those dark moments when you are trying to create something new and you find yourself in a maze of dead ends, when all seems hopeless and you feel unworthy? I did not have a ready answer. I was still trying to understand myself, especially since I feel that way so much of the time. I told her it was very difficult and it is very difficult not to despair. To look into the abyss and dance gingerly away. I have had many conversations about this sense of being simultaneously lost and found with individuals in all walks of life and with leaders in organizations, not only with artists. For leaders this is often a poignantly uncomfortable experience since leaders are paid to make sense of things.

But I believed the ability to hold these two opposing ideas—the sense of being both lost and found—is the stepping stone into creativeness. There is a deeper sensing that allows these two ideas to co-exist. I didn't know where it came from or the nature of it but it seemed to rise up when these two truths were most intensely felt.

Paris Calls

The story of this deeper sensing came to me somewhere between Normandy, France and Needham, Massachusetts several months earlier.

My wife Karen and I had gone to Paris for five weeks. Friends of ours, the Harrisons, lived in the 15th arrondissement and invited us to live in their four room apartment on a freeloader basis while they made their annual visit to family back in the States. Nat worked for Agence France-Presse as a correspondent. Margaret was a parish coordinator at the American Cathedral of the Holy Trinity, an outpost of the US Episcopal Church. We did not have specific plans while there with the exception of heading to Normandy and the Landing Beaches for five days, but felt it was too good an opportunity to pass up. So we used our accumulated points for airline tickets and prepared to immerse ourselves in *la vie Parisienne*. At $1.45 to the euro we were thankful to have free digs and a neighborhood to call home for a period. I dusted off my old copy of *A*

Moveable Feast which I had originally read sitting in the Luxembourg Garden back in 1965. After I had graduated from NYU and before starting my doctoral program I headed to Paris for six months to study with the philosopher Paul Ricoeur at the Sorbonne. Of course, back then my imagination vibrated at the thought of living the expatriate life, and I gobbled up everything I could about Hemingway, Fitzgerald, Ford Maddox Ford, Malcolm Cowley, Gertrude Stein, Alice B Toklas, Ezra Pound, Pablo Picasso, Chaim Soutine. I even romanced the idea of making a more long term go of it.

And while I returned to begin graduate school, the mood, feel and mythic glory of Paris never left, and *A Moveable Feast* captured the seduction of Paris like nothing else I had read. I returned to Paris several times in the intervening years but these trips never had the lasting hold of my first romance with the city of light. Nor did it prepare me for the entirely unexpected and profound effect it would have on me this time around.

Karen came to Paris for a specific purpose. She had been a dyed in the wool Francophobe most her life. Her father had made a harrowing escape from Poland on the last boat to leave Danzig just as the Nazi's stormed the Polish border in 1939. He almost never made it to the boat. When Polish soldiers boarded the training to conscript anyone as young as 16, he hid under the wicker straw seat. After a brief stop in England, he sailed to Panama where he lived for 8 years with a few others from his village of Lagov. He had left his young wife and brothers and sister with the intention of sending for them as soon as he had enough money. He never was reunited with his wife, siblings or parents. They all perished in Treblinka. While in Panama he learned Spanish and continued to speak it with a quirky Yiddish-Polish accent

19

his whole life. He arrived in the U.S. in 1947, proposing to Karen's mother, a native born Chicagoan, on their first date. Later, he owned a tailor shop where he hired Hispanic tailors. I often wondered what they thought of his version of their native tongue. So Karen grew up with Spanish, studied it in high school and college. She never developed a taste for the country just north of the Pyrenees nor could she forgive it for its role in deporting Jews during the war.

Until for some reason even she does not understand, she decided to study French. Whenever friends asked what got into her she just shrugged her shoulders and raised her eyebrows, indicating they would have to look elsewhere for reasons. The notion simply came to her. This is simply the way Karen works. At first I thought this might be another of her many spontaneous but short lived enthusiasms like picking up, in turn, the mandolin, the guitar, the dulcimer, and Italian. But this one turned out differently. She threw herself into it, first studying tapes on her own for a year, then taking classes at the Alliance Francaise, blasting French language CD's on our car rides and translating French comic books. Everywhere we went she carried her pocket French dictionary in the remote event we would stumble across a French phrase in some hidden corner of suburban Boston.

So Karen had come to France to practice her French. While I admired her willingness to look and sound foolish I pitied the poor French soul who entered an unsuspecting conversation with her. She would disavow any polite attempt to switch to English as she plowed headlong into the conversation. I must confess I also felt sorry for myself since it was not unusual for us to take half an hour to walk a single Paris block as she whipped out her dictionary at every sign, bus stop, and commemorative plaque we passed.

Our friends Nat and Margaret lived in an eight story brick complex built in 1920. The elevator was wrapped in elegant wrought iron with room for two people. Or one person and one suitcase. When it was in working order it creaked all the way to *etage six* where they lived. The apartment was cozy, every available space piled with shelves that held the accumulated yield of 20 years abroad. The kitchen, one and half hips wide, had all the basics including a temperamental stove—the real oven temperature having no correlation to the dial setting—and a modest sized refrigerator. I immediately fell in love with the scallop-framed, floor to ceiling windows in the apartment. They opened to a six inch balcony secured by serpentine wrought iron railings that evoked any number of Matisse paintings.

We spent our days walking Paris, starting each morning in the apartment with a brioche or croissants bought at the patisserie around the corner. Using the metro, we chewed through several *carne* of Metro tickets in a week as we rode to a different section of the city each day.

Lunch was our big meal of the day and we took it leisurely at whatever local bistro we could find, usually filling up on traditional poached salmon and overcooked vegetables, steak frites, perhaps some leg of lamb. We also tried a number of Vietnamese, Indonesian or Moroccan joints. We generally limped home by 3 or 4 in the afternoon.

I was especially looking forward to one particular walk. The destination could not be found in any guidebook. 9 Avenue de Clichy in the 9th arrondissement where in the late1860's and early 1870's the rag tag, struggling but impassioned artists soon to be known as the Impressionists gathered in the evening to discuss, debate and even duel over ideas at Café Guerbois. Edouard Manet was the central figure. But he was joined by such future giants as Claude Monet, Auguste Renoir, Frederic Bazille, Henri Fantin-Latour. The circle grew as Edgar Degas and Alfred Sisley arrived. On occasion Emile Pissarro and the unkempt Paul Cezanne showed up, the latter often directly from his studio with paint still slathered on his clothes. In these conversations the revolution in art was first proposed, tested, and mid-wifed. Of course, these same café dwellers also painted side by side *en plein air* as well as in their studios. So their banter prodded them to dab an entirely new vision on their canvases side by side, even placing strokes on each other's work and intoning each other to brighten up their "tobacco juice" colors. I had long held pictures in my mind of the place—shaped by the café paintings of Manet and Henri Toulouse-Lautrec. The café was populated with top hatted men in mutton chop beards. Smoked filled the air and red nosed, tightly corseted ladies in black dresses sipped glasses of absinth, conveying a slightly disheveled worldliness about them. And there in a far corner I could see the animated gesticulations of the impressionist pantheon generating wind currents that would change the world. Of course I would have loved to sit in one of those chairs, ears peaked, eyes dancing from one to the other, taking it all in. And, in the absence of such a possibility, to at least step into the same space they had occupied, even if more than a century and a half later. Their conversations often rose to shouting and in one case, Manet was so incensed by an unfavorable review by his friend Louis Edmond Duranty that Manet collared Duranty at the café and gave him a slap. Duranty's demands for an apology went unrequited. A few days later they showed up for a duel with swords in the Forest of Saint-Germain-en-Laye, Manet being seconded by the novelist Emile Zola and Duranty by Paul Alexis, a novelist and journalist. Manet inflicted a wound above the right breast and the seconds stepped in to declare that honor had been served. And in true French style, Manet and Duranty remained friends for the rest of their lives.

It was to this caldron of heated revolutionary creativity that we strode one beautiful day, fully evoking the blue sky and full throated clouds of a Sisley landscape.

As we emerged from the scrubby Place de Clichy Metro and headed toward number 9 my heart began to race. Karen had to hustle to keep up with me. Alas, we found ourselves in front of a modern day emporium called Athlete's World, bins of cheap sneakers spilling out into the street.

I was inconsolable, set up by the gullibility of a longing imagination. The world had moved on. In its bustle and mercantile zeal, the world I currently occupied had little room for the fantastic imaginings of a hopeless dreamer.

But there is redemption all around Paris. And for me, the artist I most wanted to spend time with was Chaim Soutine. I had learned that Musee de l'Orangerie had a large collection of his work. From the moment I first saw his paintings in a book many years earlier, before I began painting and sculpting, I was struck by their intense and unrelenting agitation combined with their hypnotically luscious colors. His yellow hues, deep greens and splashing red filled the canvas with emotion and surprise. His portraits commanded the page with their quirky expressions and odd proportions and daring use of black and ultra marine blue.

Soutine was the tenth of eleven children born into a poor orthodox Jewish tailor's family in Russia in 1893. He spent his childhood in hunger and cruelty. From an early age he was beaten and locked up, once for trading kitchen ware for crayons; another time he was beaten within an inch of his life by his own brothers for attempting to draw portraits, since according to strict tradition one was forbidden to make "graven images." It was not unusual for him to take refuge from his family in the forest.

By the time he made it to Paris in 1913 he was sickly and penniless but he found another refuge at La Ruche, the "Beehive," a warren of studios for the equally poor Diaspora of artists who found their way to Paris. These included Picasso, Modigliani, Chagall, Lipschitz. To scrape by he took odd jobs such as unloading crates of fish at Les Halles or painting posters. Through it all he persisted in his art. He hung carcasses of raw meat and painted them until even his fellow artists protested the odor. He spent hour upon hour at the Louvre, especially studying his beloved Rembrandt.

But the wolf was never far from his door. At first the lupine threat came from grinding poverty and poor health and then from the Nazis. During the war he took refuge in remote French villages until he had to make a risky and hasty return to Paris to undergo surgery for a perforated ulcer. But it was too late. He was buried in an unmarked grave for fear the Nazis would deface it.

It's hard to look at a Soutine painting without becoming mesmerized by the turbulence that engulfs it. He is said to have destroyed almost as many paintings as have survived. And the ones that have survived bear the scars of his struggle. There is a kind of raw energy to his work, worked and reworked and reworked again as though he were engaged in an argument to the death with the subject. There is something in his paintings that he is trying to exorcise and even the finished work leaves the impression that he didn't quite succeed in doing so. Perhaps the power of his painting is that even for the pieces he finished the viewer is left with a sense of ongoing-ness, with the sense that he stopped not because he believed he was finished but because he had to get on to something else.

Soutine himself recalled how as a child, "Once I saw the village butcher slice the neck of a bird and drain the blood out of it. I wanted to cry out, but his joyful expression caught the sound in my throat... ...This cry, I always feel it there. When I painted the beef carcass it was still this cry that I wanted to liberate. I have still not succeeded." Soutine's art is the long, painful, impossible slog to exorcise the cry stuck in his throat. For me it is an example of the inscrutable will to creativeness, even as I am at a loss to explain it.

Spending time with Soutine at Musee de l'Orangerie helped soothe my disappointment at seeing a discount sports emporium where the old Café Guerbois used to be. The old Beehive has gone through a remodel and today is private residences surrounded by a tall iron gate. But if you are lucky enough to stand at the gate awhile and plead with an incoming resident to allow you to at least walk the grounds you can let your imagination conjure up the dilapidated old tenement and the odor of oil paints and aging slabs of beef wafting through the air.

After our day of hoofing it around Paris, I would head over to Café Macis Muscade on Rue des Entrepreneur where I would hook up to their wireless and

25

write or email while sipping on a 1664 or la maison rouge or an Orangina. In his day Hemingway would have referred to the proprietor as Monsieur so and so. Henri—his last name never came up—was the name of my proprietor at Café Macis Muscade. After two days he acknowledged familiarity by bringing me a bowl of nuts with my drink. And after my first week he knew not to bring a second beer or glass of wine when the bottle or glass was empty. He also knew to bring another Orangina when I finished my first. Henri was tall, trim, with a bushy head of black hair. He shaved every third day and wore a big silver cowboy buckle with his jeans. We probably could have struck up a conversation about it, but that's not why I was there. Our conversation consisted of "Merci" and "je vous enpris." Every afternoon the same crowd of 40 and 50 somethings—five or six of them—gathered around a table, smoked cigarettes and kept up a lively chatter.

Karen and I came to call dinner *notre repas charmant*—"our lovely meal"—because it usually consisted of some simple fare—a baguette bought on the way home with cheese, sardines or tuna with olives from a Monoprix can. Of course there were a couple glasses of Fitou, a hearty red wine Nat had put me onto and which you could pick up on the cheap.

In some ways this made for a very dull life and one which we thoroughly enjoyed. We were in fact very un-lost generation like. Each evening Karen read her Henning Mankell mysteries and I sketched, often with Karen as my subject. I capped off the evening by reading. Nat had a wall of old books, some dating back to his college years, so I dove in at random, although I did get reunited with the very un-French Walt Whitman and kept coming back to him throughout our stay.

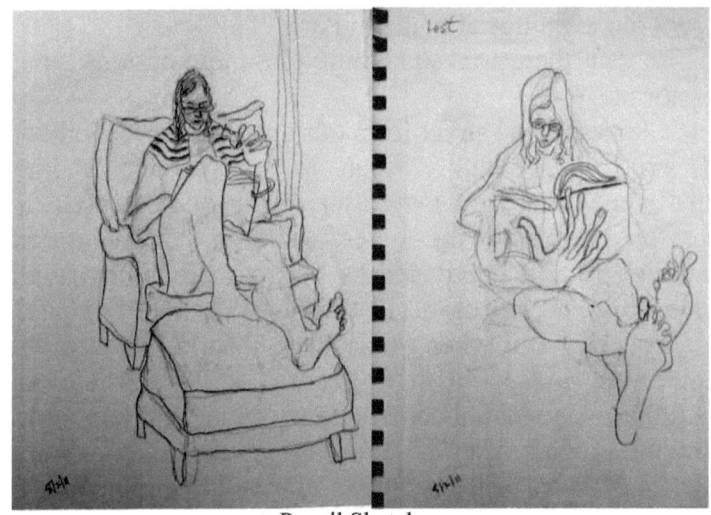
Pencil Sketches

Around 10:30 or 11 o'clock the courtyard out our window came alive. We kept the large windows open to cool off the apartment. If you looked outside you could see several folks, bare-chested or lightly clad, leaning over their railing taking their final smoke of the day. Midway through the evening the shouts arose—a group of men had gathered in one of the apartments to watch a soccer match and they eagerly shared their commentary of the action through a cacophony of yeahs and boos.

And then came the voice of Monsieur Falstaff. At least that is what we called him. His voice rang out in a piercing tenor. He would bellow on for half an hour in full throated, operatic glory. After several nights we learned he was not singing opera at all. He was in truth a madman spewing invective at the world. Of course, Karen was distraught that she had not understood what he was singing from the beginning. This was the modern symphony of sounds that served as our backdrop as we spent our evenings at home in Paris.

But there was something else quite curious going on for me.

Across the street from our apartment a scaffolding of pipes and planks began to rise around another apartment building. Day after day I would watch the scaffolding climb the outer walls of the apartment building. I was captivated by the intricate interweaving of the pipes. Up close all the pipes seemed tenuously interlocked. But when you looked from a distance you could see a steel skin beginning to encapsulate the building. How could something so flimsy and temporary looking up close appear so strong and permanent from a distance? That was a paradox that would come back to me in a surprising flash.

By the time we left for our trip to Normandy the scaffolding had risen to the third floor of the eight story apartment building. I wanted to see the Bayeux Tapestry and visit the landing beaches and the American Cemetery at Colleville Sur Mer. Three of my uncles had landed on Omaha Beach. Little could I have expected this personal pilgrimage would exert such a powerful effect on my imagination.

The Bayeux Tapestry

The Bayeux Tapestry tells the story of William the Conqueror's rise from Duke of Normandy to King of England, culminating in his victory at the Battle of Hastings in 1066, changing the course of English and French history. Today it sits behind a circular glass encasement. Its 12 inch high linen panels are sewn together to form a tapestry stretching greater than 70 yards long. The main yarn colors are terracotta or russet, blue-green, gold, olive green, and blue, with small amounts of dark blue or black. The figures are primitive, the stitching imprecise, the colors muted.

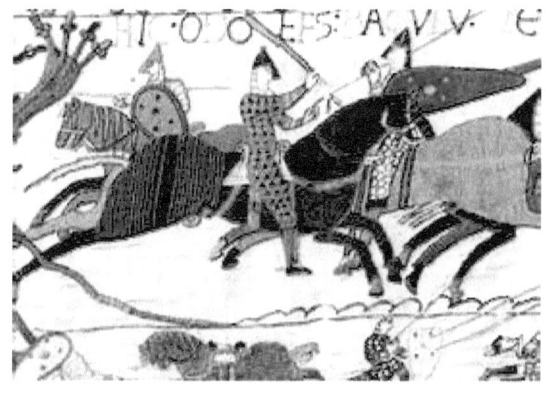

Viewing the tapestry in the darkened room, I found myself wondering how we humans would be viewing our history in the year 3000, a similar expanse of time as that between the Battle of Hastings and today, approximately 1000 years. Would our descendants be looking back with the same self satisfied belief we hold today. Would they believe it has all turned out just so, one event leading to the other until history itself flowed to their very doorstep as naturally and logically as a river flows from source to the sea. We have difficulty imagining history differently; rather we accept the contours of time and events as an unalterable path rather than a thicket of possibilities and potential offshoots that could have taken us to somewhere quite different. Great minds have tried to impose a kind of ex post facto meaning or hidden logic to history as though they were reviewing a film to identify its themes. The Greek historian Herodotus advanced the claim that all men can know equally about divine things, presenting history itself as an expression of democracy—at least the ancient Greek version. By the 18th century, German philosopher Hegel offered his dialectic in which world history was seen as "the unfolding of Spirit in time." Benedetto Croce, writing in the 20th century, spoke about history as the inevitable triumph of liberty. Of course, I have a personal affinity for Thomas Carlyle's belief that history is just "a distillation of rumors."

In fact, as exemplified by The Bayeux Tapestry, history is the work of little hands, women's hands in this case, ladies of the court, tugging at vat died yarn, recapitulating events told lip to ear and sewing them into a wool and linen epic mural. These women could barely lift their eyes beyond the immediate task of translating recent events into visual form to say nothing of gazing 1000 years into their future. And if they could engage in such conjuring, even their imaginations could not have come close to picturing our world. We possess no less faulty imaginations. Despite our wealth of information, our technology, our advances in understanding the nature of human cognition, our hubris, we are no more able to see into such a future as could our ladies of the tapestry in 1066.

I pictured these ladies working, singing, whispering, gossiping. Hands and mouths and imaginations in a buzz of activity. And yet such busy-ness could not disguise an essential loss. There is a gap between the actual experience they are describing and the description itself. Between the people and events as they were experienced and the primitive figures sewn into linen fabric representing those events. Between the actual and the remembered. Between what happened and what is told. Proust was right when he said

"Remembrance of things past is not necessarily the remembrance of things as they were."

We are touched by experience, by history and then they are gone. They take some other form, perhaps memory, perhaps a tapestry or a poem or a painting or a photograph, but even in their new form they cannot replicate the original experience in its intensity, it richness, its multi-sensory, fleeting truth. We cannot escape this melancholy dimension of being alive. Even when we recall our happiest experiences we are simultaneously stirred by the melancholy of its incompleteness. I wonder if this paradox is not an impetus for art. As imperfect as it is at least art gives us something to hold onto, to affirm, to remind us of the glory and imperfection of our humanity.

So what an amazing gift these ladies have left us, this chronicle of real events, photo shopped as it might be by the technology of its time, embellished in the telling. And yet, as provocative as the Bayeux Tapestry was in highlighting the sweep of human events the tapestry left me in a state of great agitation. There was something in the gap between events as they occurred and the telling of those events that began to claw at me. I did not know what it was. It caused great discomfort. It opened the possibility that we live lies in so far as we live our lives based upon memories. I could not let go of this possibility and its implications. But I could not have anticipated that as strong as this sense of agitation was it would not match the one I experienced during my visit to the American Cemetery at Colleville-sur-Mer, also known as Omaha Beach.

Omaha Beach

Pilgrims from all over the world spill into the sprawling parking lot of the American Cemetery at Omaha Beach and I was one of them. Like many others I had a connection to Omaha Beach. All six of my uncles fought in WWII, all returning. Three of them landed at Omaha Beach. Fortunately, they came ashore on the second day of the invasion after the fiercest fighting and slaughter had happened.

Early memories began to play in my mind as we made our way toward the pavilion. I was 5 years old when Uncle Hy came to take me shopping on Pitkin Avenue in Brooklyn. I remember him holding my hand as we walked down the crowded street lined with shops. Creaky wooden fish stalls piled high with whole fish and ice. Cages with clucking chickens. And damp pickle barrels I thought as thick and tall as sequoias. Uncle Hy liked to banter and he was bantering away when a loud blast from a backfiring car shot through the air. Uncle Hy threw me to the ground and hunched over me for what seemed like an interminable period of time. I could hardly breathe from his bear like mass and the heavy coat that smothered me. I was scared out of my wits, feeling the air sucked out of me. Uncle Hy brushed the street off me and gave me a hug. He asked if I was hurt, his eyes glazed, furtively looking around. The scare wouldn't leave me. Even when Uncle Hy took my hand again I felt myself still shaking inside. We continued on our walk, only now without the banter. Uncle Hy never said anything about the incident when we got home. Nor did I. Years later I learned that Uncle Hy had had some "after-effects" from the war.

Hy worked as a train operator for the NYC subway system for more than 40 years. He lived into his eighties and later on had taken to going on long walks. By then he had moved down to Del Ray Beach in Florida with my Aunt Florence. He would disappear for hours and I often wondered what he thought about on those walks. I wondered if his thoughts called up muddy foxholes and lost comrades or if his mind cried for his teenage daughter who was crushed by a car years later. Or perhaps further back to growing up in Sioux City, Iowa before moving to New Jersey and then Brownville in Brooklyn with the family. I also couldn't help but wonder if any of his thoughts carried him back to that incident with his little nephew or had the recollection of it faded into the murky swamp of forgotten memories.

My closest tie to Omaha Beach came from my Uncle Eddie. Eddie was the youngest of six in the family and my mom was the second youngest. They were close. He called my mom "Kiddo" which I didn't quite understand since everyone else called her Helen, or Hindela—her Yiddish diminutive. I still have copies of the v-letters he wrote from the war asking how "little Freddie" was doing. I was six months old when he headed off for basic training. Family lore has it that when Eddie came to say goodbye, he leaned over the crib to kiss me and I peed in his face.

Eddie was a looker. He had dark wavy hair, a ripped physique and movie star features. He was also a wheeler dealer with mischief in his eyes. He had been wounded on the push into Germany and met a fellow soldier in the hospital who introduced him to the business side of the black market. Years later Eddie opened up about selling wine, cigarettes, lingerie during the war. Returning to the states he became a cutter in the garment business. He also brought back Nazi war loot, including a copy of Mein Kampf. It's not clear how Eddie got his hands on the book. The version I came to know was that he had taken the copy from the rucksack of a dead German soldier. Years later we learned that wasn't true although we never did learn how he did come by it. For years I kept the book on our bookshelf in an upside down position among my Jewish books. It was a small act of defiance.

That book also acted as a constant reminder of those distant events. At one point I considered giving it to a university library or research center. In truth, I never really looked at the book in a serious way. There was a photo of a young, menacing looking Hitler on the inside. I remember several times over the years taking the book out and glaring back at that photo. But that is as far as my examination went. When my children learned of my intention they became upset, claiming that the book had become part of family history and I could not give it away. I sensed that the book in some strange and perverse way connected them to people they could never know. The next time my daughter Hinda came home she opened the cover to find an inscription. I had never paid much attention to it. My son Jacob had lived in Berlin for several years and had become fluent in German so Hinda showed the inscription to him. The book was given to Walter and Clara Jess "on the occasion of your wedding by the Mayor of Lubeck."

Hinda's initial journalistic curiosity about the copy of Mein Kampf turned into an obsession. She felt compelled to learn more about the Jess family. Armed with her brother's translation of the inscription, she hired a genealogist in Germany to track down information about Walter Jess. She herself made a trip to Lubeck and the city's archives. She learned that Walter Jess had joined the National Socialist Party in 1933 and had been a ranking officer in the Wehrmacht. She also discovered that he had survived the war and moved from Lubeck to Mains where he died in 1967. Along the way he had three children, two of whom were still alive, one living in Germany and the other in New York City. This information, of course, called into question the family's story of how Eddie had gotten hold of the book. According to the Jess daughter, she has a memory of American soldiers entering her house and trashing the bookshelves. Perhaps Eddie was one of them? Perhaps he traded for the book on the black market? We now knew that the story of Eddie taking the book from a dead Walter Jess could not be true, but we had no story with which to replace it.

My pilgrimage to Omaha Beach grew in part out of my need to get closer to my uncles' experience. By then, all of my uncles had died. So when I entered the pavilion and saw the photos of young soldiers it was as though I was turning the pages of our own family album.

The pavilion is made of concrete and glass and overlooks the landing beach below. The stark interior is empty of all artifacts or furniture. The walls are filled with photos of soldiers, in some cases up close, smiling, in other cases in battle on D-Day, and in still other cases wounded or dead. Footage from old newsreels tell the story of the D-Day landing, the arduous preparations, the intricate planning, the unpredictable weather, the fateful decisions. Photo after photo is accompanied by a brief biographical background of the soldiers and their acts of remarkable heroism. Most of the photos are of soldiers who never returned. Visitors shuffle along the walls slowly, stopping, looking, reading. They move along silently. Every once in while you hear the muffled heaves of someone sobbing.

When you step onto the cemetery grounds you find yourself confronted by lush grass and a reverential quiet. Not a single pilgrim speaks. Rows and rows of gleaming white crosses with an occasional Star of David, in perfect symmetry, stretch in every direction. Nine thousand three hundred and eighty seven soldiers lay here. The names of another 1557 missing soldiers are written on the memorial wall. The cemetery stands on a bluff with Omaha Beach below, the waves gently lapping at the shore.

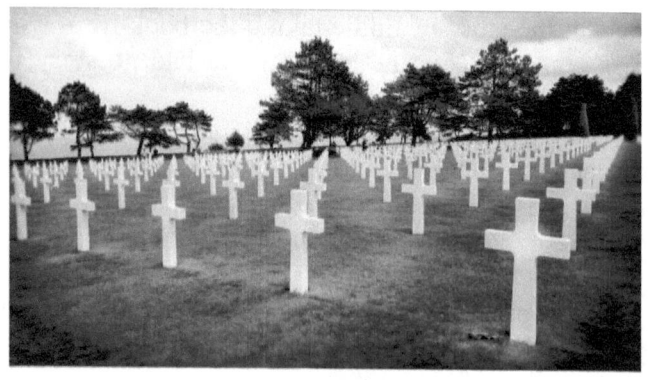

Standing in the middle of the cemetery I was overwhelmed with an indescribably sense of loss. I was overcome by deep sobbing. I felt my body heaving with emotion. I couldn't stop. I allowed myself to surrender to the stupendous sense of emptiness inside. It seemed the only possible response and I had to let it run its course.

There is a wonderful children's story called The Treasure. The story tells of a poor man in a remote village who has a dream in which a voice comes to him and tells him to go to the capital city where he will find a vast treasure. The man ignores the voice and goes about eking out his daily living. This dream is followed by another in which the voice grows louder. The man ignores the dream again, but the third night the voice is so loud and strident that the man leaves his village. He travels a great distance over mountain and river until he arrives at the gates of the capital city where he is confronted by a guard. The man tells the guard his story in hopes he will allow him to pass into the city, but he is greeted by loud guffaws. The guard tells the poor man that "If I listened to every dream I had I would go to a small village in the mountains and go to an old house and look under the hearth and I would find a vast treasure. Now go back home!" The poor man heeds the guard's advice, makes the trek back to his village and digs a hole by his hearth where he finds a vast treasure. He then places a sign above his door which reads: Sometimes we must travel far to find what is near.

An Idea

The story of the poor man played on me as I tried to come to terms with the experience of my visit to the American Cemetery and more broadly my time in France. The agitation I felt after the Bayeux Tapestry turned into a kind of deep reflection about time, memory and loss. Not only the sense of profound loss I felt at Omaha Beach but the effects of time on memory. I began to think that memory was less an act of recall, or a product of brain physiology than it was an act of creative expression. It is through memory that we create ourselves. Through the arranging and rearranging of memories, overlaid by stories, we construct a rich imaginative narrative that describes who we are to ourselves and others. At a broader social level we call this history. But it was not until we returned to Paris and I noticed that the scaffolding had fully wrapped itself around the apartment building across from us that I came to think of the notion of constructing a new imaginative scaffolding that could potentially house memories both lost and found, experienced and imagined. Memory called and I thought that in the Bayeux Tapestry and Omaha Beach I had found the scaffolding on which to reclaim what was in danger of being lost. I decided to refer to it as Chronicle, in honor of the spirit of the Bayeux Tapestry as a chronicle of its time.

The notion was simple in concept. I would make a series of paintings in images that captured the events and memories of the first five years of my life. The series would represent my effort to preserve what was in danger of being irrevocably lost in the darkness of time. It was my attempt to leave a finger print in the form of brush strokes. I needed to wrestle with the dilemma of the relationship between original experience and the memory of that experience, between original events and a description of those events. It was an opportunity to explore storytelling and the formation of myth. With Omaha Beach and the Bayeux Tapestries now in the rear view mirror, but still alive in my imagination, I began to think about art as diary and our refusal to surrender to the mists of time.

I wrote in my sketchbook: "How the hell am I going to do this?"

I returned to the Café Macis Muscade on Rue des Entrepreneurs only one more time. In some ways I wanted to remain in Paris. I also felt the pull to return to the States to begin working on this new project. Yet I could not help recall the paradox of home and distance that was so much in play in Hemingway's early writing. He could see his early childhood more clearly from Paris. He could capture growing up in Michigan with greater vividness by removing himself from the very setting. As in The Treasure, Hemingway traveled far to uncover what was near. It reminded me of the great Rembrandt painting of The Artist in His Studio. The artist stands reverentially some distance from the easel. An eerie glow emanates from the canvas. Yet, the distance provides a perspective he could not realize while standing up close and engaged with the painting. Hemingway needed distance, a different cultural filter to better comprehend, to better capture what was most true of what was closest to him. And so too the painter according to Rembrandt. Again I bumped up against paradox. We see something more clearly by removing ourselves from what is seen. By this time I had become reacquainted with Leaves of Grass from Nat's bookshelf. The poem oozes with energy and exultation. Ideas and provocations vibrate in every line. I had the sense that Whitman piles EVERYTHING into his poetry.

> *Do I contradict myself?*
> *Very well, then I contradict myself,*
> *I am large, I contain multitudes.*

His poetry had a great effect on me and at one point I noted in my sketchbook that I would like to paint like Whitman wrote poetry—everything in.

In fact, it was while sitting in the Café Macis Muscade on my last visit there that I read a passage from Song of Myself. I had been playing with a thought after my visit to Bayeux and Omaha Beach, reflecting on memories of my uncles in Brooklyn and the power they held over me and wondering what I would now see when I returned home and opened our old family albums. The thought kept running through my mind:

Art is an encounter with the unseen in the seen. This is a paradox.

And this must be so I told myself. What happens below the visible surface precedes even the act of picking up a paint brush. It is there and then that the initial idea, the initial encounter, the initial tension begins to take form. It's where the imagination plays and seduces. It guides the hand that creates what the eye ultimately sees above the surface, on the canvas. In some sense these thoughts were an abstraction since I had not really begun to work on Chronicle. It was all simply an idea. And then my eyes took in the following passage:

Clear and sweet is my soul, and clear and sweet is all that is not my soul.

Lack one lacks both, and the unseen is proved by the seen, Till that becomes unseen and receives proof in its turn.

Whitman had taken my thought into a virtuous circle of paradox. The seen and unseen are ying and yang. They validate each other. They are both part of a larger, mysterious, messy truth. We cannot separate them. Without one, the other disappears. The visible world disappears without the unseen world. The unseen is the scaffolding that holds up the seen.

40

A question for me was how to express the unseen world through the seen world.

All This I See In Myself

The great essayist Montaigne lays himself and us bare:

All contradictions may be found in me by some twist and in some fashion. Bashful, insolent, chaste, lascivious, talkative, taciturn, tough, delicate, clever, stupid, surly, affable, lying, truthful, learned ignorant, liberal, miserly, and prodigal: all this I see in myself to some extent depending on how I turn; and whoever studies himself really attentively finds in himself, yes, even in his judgment, this gyration and this discord. I have nothing to say about myself absolutely, simply and solidly, without confusion and without mixture, or in one word.

Montaigne puts us on notice: the very self is paradox.

We live as much in paradox as fish live in water.

Nor can we escape from the most fundamental paradox of all.

We are born to die.

All creativity grows from this lumpy paradox.

We behold and tremble before our mortality much like Rilke did before the rose: "oh, pure contradiction."

Mortality is friend and foe and at this intersection roils up our undeniable compulsion to create, to leave an evidence, to cry out that we are here, have been here, remain alive.

On the other side of mortality stands the possibility of emptiness.

To be human is to be incapable of accepting emptiness.

A Zen koan reads:

When the question is common
The answer is also common.

When the question is sand in a bowl of boiled rice
The answer is a stick in the soft mud.

We are the stick in the soft mud of existence. I am reminded of the story of Henri Gautier-Brzeska, a young sculptor of great promise, a friend and contemporary of the great sculptor Jacob Epstein. He had already created over 120 sculptures and 2000 works on paper by the time he enlisted in the French army at the age of 22 at the outset of WWI.

In letters from the front he describes the day-to-day scene around him. "Human masses teem and move, are destroyed and crop up again. Horses are worn out in three weeks, die by the roadside. Dogs wander, are destroyed and others come along. The bursting shells, the volleys, wire entanglements, projectors, motors, the chaos of battle do not alter in the least the outlines of the hill we are besieging." Gautier-Brzeska fought hand to hand. Corpses laid for days in the wasteland between the two encampments.

At one point he wrestles a mauser from a German soldier and takes it back to his trench during a break in the battle. In one of his letters, he reflects: "Its heavy unwieldy shape swamped me with a powerful image of brutality. I was in doubt for a long time whether it pleased or displeased me. I found I did not like it. I broke the butt off and with my knife I carved in it a design with which I tried to express a gentler order of feeling which I preferred." How can we explain this side by side capacity for brutality and gentleness? This paradox of forming beauty from ugliness? To destroy life and give birth to it?

In the midst of devastation and human degradation, the young Gaudier-Brzeska finds it within himself to reconfigure a weapon of killing into a "gentler order."

Two months after he sent this letter, Gaudier-Brzeska is killed in battle. He is 23 years old.

Gautier-Brzeska is a stick in the soft mud of existence.

So Much As Never Lived

And so we flew home. I had felt increasingly antsy at not engaging directly with paint and canvas, scratching, pushing, pulling that is part of the actual painting process. In Paris I had sketched in my sketchbook and made notes but I hadn't done a lick of painting. In truth, I still am a novice so the idea of going a long period without painting ate at me. I could take momentary solace in Wyeth's idea that "I dream a lot. I do more painting when I'm not painting. It's in the subconscious." But that could only take me so far. The rest was rationalization.

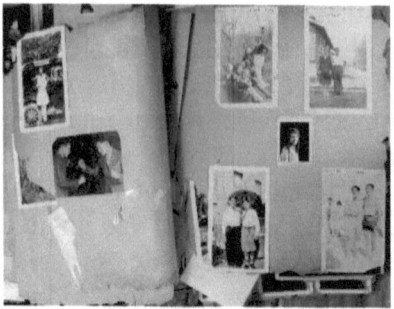 The first thing I did upon arriving home was leaf through the old family photo album. Its brittle pages nearly crumbled at my touch. Some of the photos date back to 1919. But I had the sense that I was looking at these images for the first time. I had spent hours in the past looking through the album, even wondering about the stories behind the photos. This time, though, was different. I couldn't help but feel I was staring at people whose stories would be lost to time if I didn't find a way to preserve them. Even worse. If I did not paint them they would so much as never have lived. If I painted them they would be both dead and alive.

Studio Space

My studio is part studio, part office. It is an extension of a section of the basement in the back of my house, located on an entirely pleasant, innocuous tree lined suburban street. In order to get to the studio I go down a set of back stairs and through an unfinished part of the basement we use for storing things. Once in the studio I can stare out the stairwell and see the sky and beyond my backyard to a Scotch Pine, Norway spruce, oak, some maple, and just on the other side of my detached garage a ragged looking Ailanthus tree, kin to the tree made famous in the book *A Tree Grows in Brooklyn.* My desk and computer sit at one end of the

44

studio, tucked in a small alcove with a small rectangular window high on the wall peeking out toward the driveway. I can see across the room to my painting space. It is not unusual for me to be on the phone while looking at a painting in progress. After completing a call I can take the few steps across the room and into a different universe where I can begin to work on the painting again.

In another corner of the studio is a sink, by now coated with layers of crusted paint—washed and scrubbed to no avail—evidence of the glacial struggle to become an artist. Rounding out the four corners of the studio, sit two large stuffed chairs that have hosted many conversations, at times comforting or poignant or disconcerting or tearful or uplifting, sometimes all at once. They are—one in red and blue denim plaid, the other in yellow and blue striped denim—cushioned sentinels to the whispered vulnerabilities of myself and others.

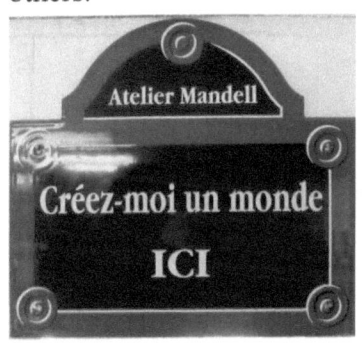 While in Paris I had a sign made that said *Creez-Moi un monde ici*. (Create me a world here.) I hung the sign over the French doors that bring light in from the south. The sign is a way of holding myself accountable to the project. I cannot escape seeing it every day. We all play tricks on ourselves in order to keep on the path, to keep on trucking—that eventually lead to a state of creativeness— despite the distractions both internal and external. Placing "Atelier Mandell" above the door was my effort to call my own bluff, to place a clear sign

post, a kind of amulet to warn any potential dis-enablers that this was a serious place, not devoid of laughter and joy, but dedicated nonetheless to a worthy aspiration.

Each morning Karen left me a cup of tea on the table in my studio. She unpredictably varied the type of tea, sometimes oolong, sometimes genmaicha, sometimes PJ Tips, sometimes green or barley or Constant Comet (from our "graduate school days"). Regardless, each morning the tea inevitably turned cold before I got to it. Later in the morning, when she asked how I liked the tea I told her it was refreshing. She shook her head with an unspoken but knowing rebuke in her eyes. She knew the drill, but she kept her end of the bargain. Tea helps you live longer, she never tired of reminding me. *Women's World* tells her this and many other secrets to living well and longer. Every morning she left me the same brown cup, bought many years ago from Bennington Pottery.

Facing the Blank Canvas for the First Time

I knew from the beginning that I didn't want to paint on stretched canvas. Partly because I didn't know how much canvas I would need as the work would unfold. I built a frame to support a large canvas measuring 7 feet by 10 feet. But when I attempted to attach the canvas the entire structure tumbled down on me.

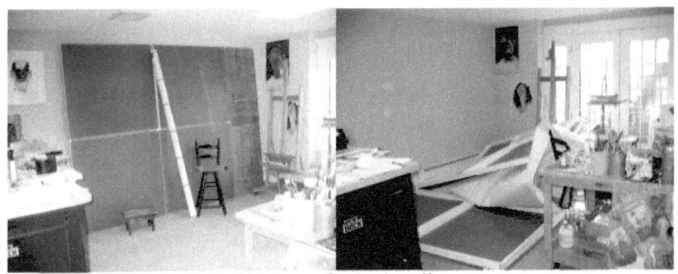
Photos of My Studio

I wanted the flexibility of creating different panels that would allow for the evolution (expansion) of the work and for the incorporation of written words and phrases. In the end I simply cut pieces of canvas, tacked them to the wall and began painting.

So I am staring at a blank canvas. The canvas is primed but not stretched and clipped to the smooth side of a hard board. This is the beginning. The very first moment, before placing a stroke on the canvas, I am alone. No one is watching. I have images in mind. I had, in fact, sketched them in my sketchbook. I am envisioning a thicket of images that tell the story of the year I came into the world. 1942.

I have read how Matisse would break out in a sweat whenever he started a new painting. It is difficult to imagine a master painter such as Matisse being so unnerved, yet I could guess what was in play here. He had spent years dedicated to developing his art, stepping away from accolades he had earned in Paris to go to remote Brittany and then down to Collioure in the south, making dramatic shifts in direction, introducing the brilliant colors that would lead to the founding of the Fauve Movement. No matter how many reinventions, there was no guarantee that the next wouldn't be a flop. He felt he was beginning anew with each painting and dreaded repeating himself. The greater his reputation the stronger the terror, in his eyes, his work was never good enough. His biographer tells how Matisse, even after he had earned an international reputation and had established his greatness, would drop in at a local school's live model drawing class to keep sharp and honest. I can only imagine what the unsuspecting students might have thought.

While this was comforting to a novice such as myself, I had other reasons to break into a sweat. How could I reconcile the fact that I had little formal training and limited knowledge of technique with my aspiration to express myself visually? How dare I try such a lofty undertaking with such untested skills? I couldn't help but wrestle with this dilemma. Do I defer my aspiration to begin this project until I had developed some degree of facility over the techniques I would need in order to execute the project? In fact, I was such a novice that I did not even know what techniques I would need in order to pull it off. And how might this lack of experience influence my artistic choices? Would I intentionally avoid certain techniques for fear I didn't know them or would be bad at them? And at the end of the day, even if

I did muddle my way through these techniques, did I not risk looking foolish or inadequate? Would my noble aspirations stumble over the limitations of my talent? The greatest risk, of course, was not that the world would be displeased with my work but rather such a public reaction would cause me to consider myself a failure. Yet, if I did not make the attempt, what would I think of myself? If I plunged ahead I risked producing bad art, so that standing pat seemed like the safe thing to do. Standing pat would inoculate me from all those nasty possibilities.

But then there is this mirror thing. It is difficult to ignore the mirror. The mirror is the ultimate arbiter of the choices we make. The mirror is certainly a reflection of who we are in the here and now, but it also forces us to glimpse the future. It calls out, not who is the fairest of them all, but who do you wish to be looking at in the years to come.

And the mirror would not allow me to stay on this side of the risk. I could not guarantee how I would feel on the other side but I did know how I felt on this day.

Alberto Giacometti:

> *It all means little,*
> *all the painting, sculpture, drawing,*
> *writing, or rather literature,*
> *it all has its place and nothing more.*
>
> *An attempt is everything,*
> *How marvelous!*

Interlude

A youthful Picasso approaches Rembrandt who is in his later years.

"Are we to paint what's on the face, what's inside the face, or what's behind it? Isn't that the great question?" Picasso inquires of the master.

"Painting is the grandchild of nature. It is related to God," Rembrandt responds.

"Art is a lie that helps us to realize the truth," Picasso counters.

"Painting is not made to be sniffed," Rembrandt comes back.

"Painting is just another way of keeping a diary," claims Picasso.

"The smell of paint would annoy you," Rembrandt insists.

"Every act of creation is first of all an act of destruction," Picasso persists.

"Of course you will say that I ought to be practical and ought to try and paint the way they want me to paint. Well, I will tell you a secret. I have tried and I have tried very hard, but I can't do it. I just can't do it! And that is why I am just a little crazy," Rembrandt acknowledges.

"Art washes from the soul the dust of everyday life." Picasso nods.

They bow toward each other and smile.

(These are actual quotes from Picasso and Rembrandt assembled, rearranged and disguised as a conversation.)

1942

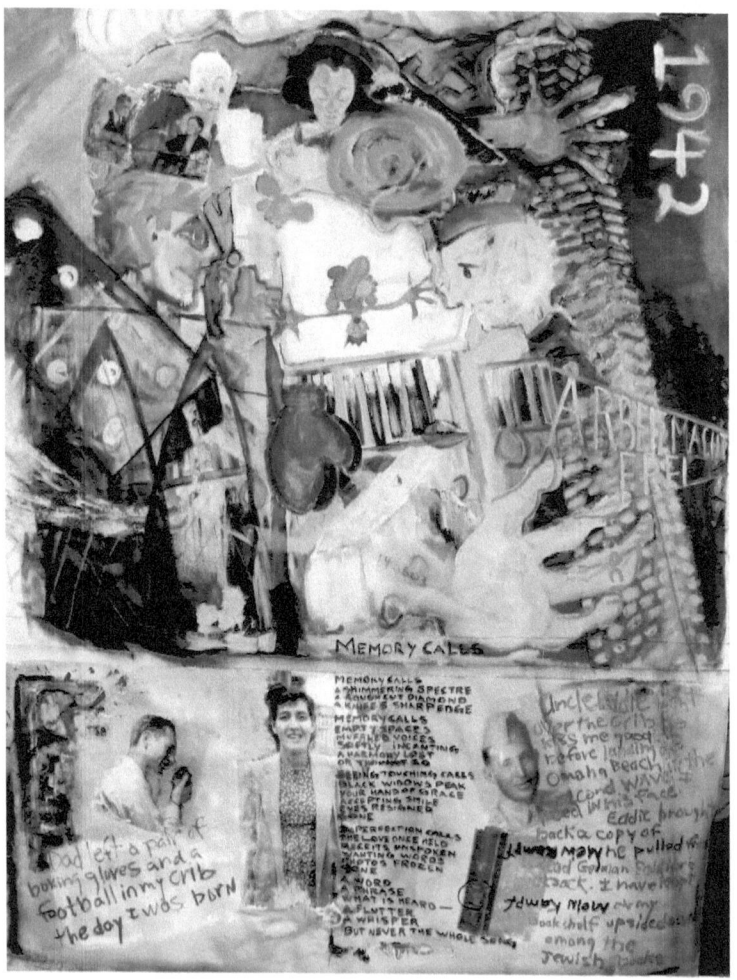

1942 was the first and most painful panel I worked on. Every stroke of these paintings represent, not only an effort to tell a story but to engage in a conversation with people and events in the past. In effect, every stroke brought me back to open wounds, to words never spoken. My mother had died of cancer at the age of 53 and my father at age 55, also of cancer. They were, of course, too young. They had unfinished business with each other as I had with each of them. My head still swam with a kaleidoscope of vivid images of them. I had lived much of my adult life believing that I would not make it past age 55 myself. I have been in a state of peculiar anticipation ever since I crossed to the other side of that line.

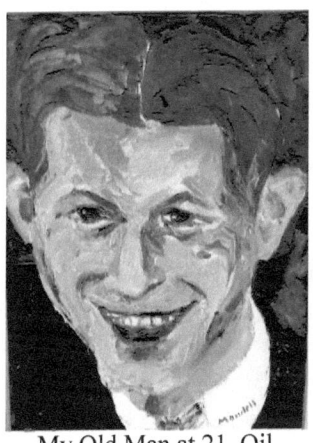 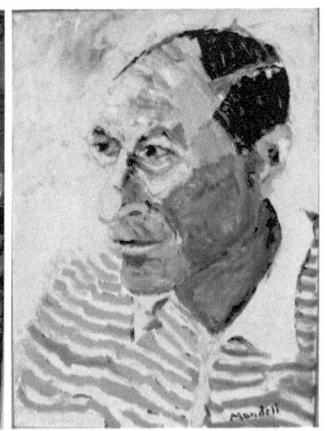

My Old Man at 21, Oil   My Old Man, Later, Oil

In earlier paintings I had made portraits of my father, each from old photos. The first I titled My Old Man at 21 in which I tried to capture his mischievous exuberance at an earlier time.

The second painting titled My Old Man, Later caught him the year he died, his eyes deflected away from the camera, staring somewhere else, showing the effects of time and my mother's absence. I had only started painting at age 58, older than my parents when they died. It was strange to think that I was making these paintings without them ever knowing that painting was in me.

The two paintings of my father turned into extended conversations with him and, in many instances, into extended stretches of shared silence. My father was not known as a big talker and over the years he became even less so. When my mom died I believe the experience of loss turned into a large dark knot of melancholy that circled his heart and ultimately choked him altogether. We would sit together for long periods not saying anything but needing each other's company. We loved each other deeply but our way of expressing it was simply by being together.

Up until the time I began Chronicle I had only painted two images of my mother. I had resisted any impulse to undertake a painting of her until that time. I am unable to explain this inability, or unwillingness. I had always held my mom with saintly reverence. In fact, one of the very first pieces of art I created was a bronze sculpture inspired by my sister Judy's oil sketch of my mom. I called it End of Day.

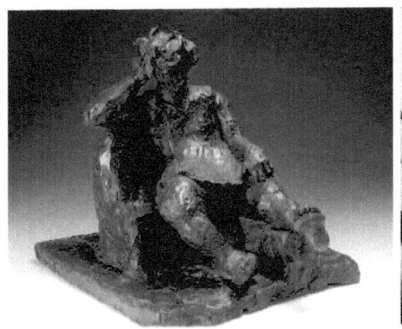
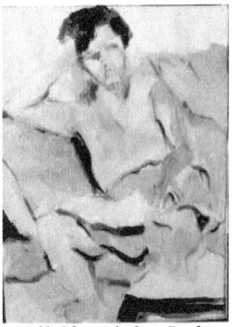

Bronze   Oil Sketch by Judy

This piece has great meaning for me since it not only draws on Judy's painting, caught in real time, but it captures an actual moment when my mom was near her end yet had not given in despite the toll the cancer had taken on her. In both Judy's painting and my sculpture, my mother's gaze is deflected away from the viewer, perhaps inward, where she was beginning to spend more of her time.

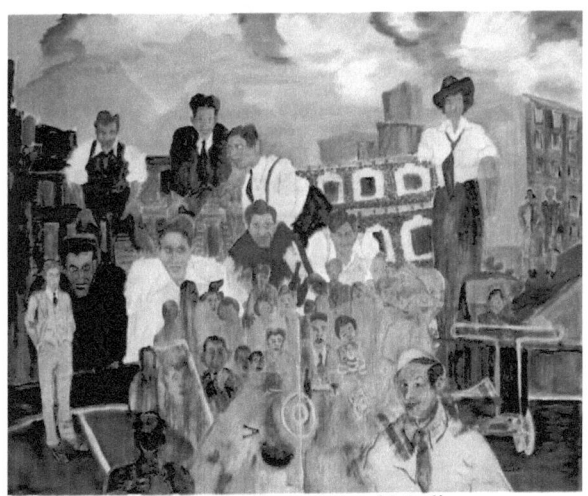

Oil with Collage, Mixed Media

The first painting in which my mother appears was part of a larger painting entitled Helen's Roof, 1933. This painting drew on a number of elements including an old photo on the side of which was handwritten the words "Helen's roof" along with the date 1933. I also collaged a number of other elements onto the painting. But perhaps the most telling element in that piece is the crisscrossing of red thread that I sewed into the canvas across my mother's breast. The overall mood I tried to create with the piece was a kind of idyllic urban nostalgia betrayed by the red sutures of future events.

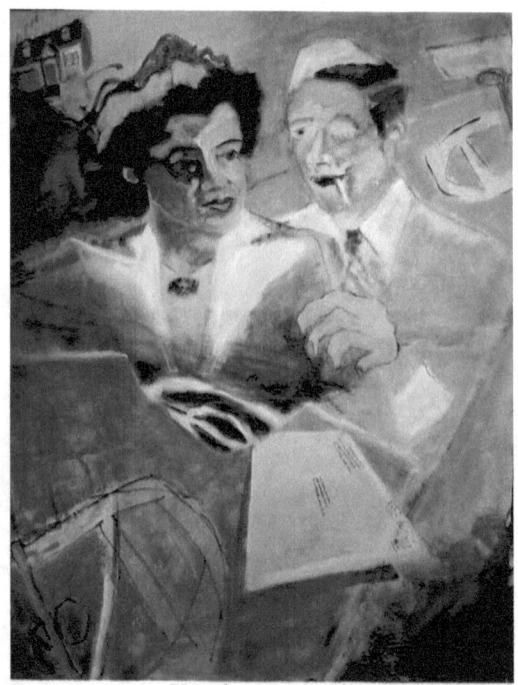

Utterby Road, Oil

The second painting with my mom in it is called Utterby Road. It is a painful piece filled with a lot of anger. At the time I was under the spell of de Kooning so I took the color palette from his early paintings. I also incorporated memories of visits I would make to my Dad's 11th floor office at 34th Street and 7th Avenue where he had his accounting practice. I would make paper airplanes and throw them out the window at the unsuspecting crowds below. In the painting, I took great care to note his return address on the envelope and to capture the postmark and stamp of an actual letter I had kept. I felt it was important to show the information on the envelope since that was where we began the promise of our suburban experience. I painted the postage stamp with Ike and the date and both my Dad's business address and our address at 134 Utterby Road, Malverne 10565.

Aside from those two paintings I didn't know how to paint my mom without overlaying my sentimentalism onto the painting. I think certain things are ineffable. The only way to paint her was to get beyond that lock of ineffability—the sense that my mom was a subject too sacrosanct to approach. I did try several sketches but in the end I could not make it happen. I simply wasn't there yet.

My mother has always remained part ghost and part living presence, calling from somewhere in the dark, soft realm of another world and whispering vivid words into my all too susceptible ears. In the studio I could sense her in the present moment even though she had been gone for over 40 years. How can that be? She had had this gift, this quality when you were with her of conveying the sense that you were the only person in the world. It was an unconditional embrace whose reach, even now, would not surrender her presence in my life.

She brought this gift to others and I think it was simply a manifestation of something at her core—a profound empathy for others, a deep sense of justice—that carried her to positions of leadership in her community. She had been president of the sisterhood at Malverne Jewish Center and of Hadassah in New York. But she reached beyond even those positions and played an instrumental role in focusing attention on civil rights in the 1950s well before it became emblazoned in the headlines a decade later. Malverne was the first northern community to be the target of a Supreme Court ruling forcing the desegregation of a school. My mom joined with other community leaders to support the implementation of a desegregation plan. Her sense of social justice imprinted itself on me. I felt compelled to head south in the summer of 1968 and march with Jesse Jackson at the commemoration of Medgar Evers' assassination. I was waylaid one night by two Louisiana troopers and brought into the woods where they radioed some of their local citizens to pay me a visit. But before the dust of the trooper car could settle I had hoofed it back to the road where I hid in the bushes and watched a truck with three men drive down the dirt road on which the troopers had left me a mile up. As soon as they passed, I put out my thumb—by now it was barely dawn— and a postal worker picked me up and drove me into Shreveport.

I can still see the salty flecks of dust shimmering in the shafts of light at New York Memorial Hospital on December 22, 1967. The doctor came in and told my Dad and me that Mom had 6 months to live. My Dad's body folded in on itself as he sunk into the chair. I was numb and had no idea what I was feeling. I think that's the moment the dream of Long Island came to its silent, sudden end. And the dance of love and deceit and code words and complicity began.

Before leaving the room my father insisted I pledge never to let my Mom know that her condition was terminal. He did not want her give up hope. He would bear the burden of the truth. And he naturally thought I was capable of doing the same.

I remember the first time I saw my mom after hearing the doctor's prognosis. Her quiet words of determination seemed at that point to support my father's instincts. But truth has a way of finding the fissures of human frailty. Sometimes it goes underground for a while, lodges itself in some hidden shadows. But truth surrounds deceit, squeezes it, until deceit has no way out except through the agony of exposure. My Dad held it in until that August night in 1968 when I received a call in Chicago that he had suffered a massive heart attack. I flew back home to find him in intensive care. He pulled me to him and whispered, "One day, I only want to live one day longer than your mother."

I remember hearing my mother talking to her friend Mary Diamond as they sat in the living room. She had already lived 12 months longer than the doctors had forecast. But the cancer had spread. She was growing weaker. I had been upstairs but as I descended the carpeted steps I began to pick up their conversation.
I paused at the bottom fully cognizant of the fact that they were unaware of my presence on the other side of the wall. I listened. My mother confided her fears in Mary. She knew the nature of her condition despite the fact that she could not get anything from her doctor or my father. She was not aware that my father had persuaded the doctor to join in the conspiracy of deceit. And she refused to put her children on the spot by asking them what they

knew about her condition. So she was left to intuit the truth. She told Mary of her fears, of her concerns for her children and for Mandy, as my Dad was called.

And then she spoke these words: "If anything happens, go to Freddie. You can always count on Freddie."

I was devastated.

Then one day in an act of frustration and anger I splashed globs of bright cadmium red on the canvas and began to work from there. In retrospect I realized the only way to artistically represent my mother was to go through the rage I felt about the ravaging of her body by the disease and of my failure to share the painful truth of her condition. By literally attacking the canvas with the red paint I was going through the motion of trying—as hopeless as it might be—to exorcise her disease, to mend her, even years later and to ask forgiveness. Ultimately the image of my mother that emerged was one which not only gave birth to me, but one which showed the raw, pink hole in her chest.

The other aspect of my mother's image that stood out for me was her widow's peak. It was the widow's peak that led me to change the title of the overall series of paintings. The process of painting triggered word fragments that kept playing in my head—"knife's edge," "muffled voices," "eyes resigned"—that formed into a call to write a poem expressing a certain longing. This longing ultimately formed into the words *Memory Calls* and tipped me into that place of love, loss and deceit that surrounded my mother's illness and death. My father had made me and my sisters pledge never to let my mother know that the doctors had told us her condition was terminal. We never broke that promise and my mother in her knowing way never let on that despite the secrecy she really understood the seriousness of her condition. Even to the end. And so a kind of code language developed among us that never allowed us the opportunity to say goodbye. I think this also explains some of the anger and blindness in Suburbs.

I wrote the poem and incorporated it into the painting:

> *Memory calls,*
> *A shimmering specter,*
> *A rough cut diamond,*
> *A knife's sharp edge.*
>
> *Memory calls,*
> *Empty spaces,*
> *Muffled voices,*
> *Softly incanting,*
> *A harmony lost,*
> *Or thought so.*
>
> *Seeing, touching calls,*
> *Black widow's peak,*
> *Your hand of grace,*
> *Accepting smile,*
> *Eyes resigned.*
> *Gone.*
>
> *Imperfection calls,*
> *The love once held,*
> *Deceits unspoken,*
> *Wanting words,*
> *Photos frozen.*
> *Gone.*

A word,
A phrase,
What is heard —
A flutter,
A whisper,
But never the whole song.

Somewhere between writing the poem and painting it into the painting I decided to change the title of the series from *Chronicle* to *Memory Calls*.

I then began to work quickly laying in other images, one after another, in a fever of motion and memory, images I associated with the year 1942, even though, as a newborn such memories were impossible. My earliest true memory is having my tonsils taken out at the age of two. I have a mental picture of lying on an ironing board in the hospital and someone placing a metal device over my nose and mouth that looked like part of a coffee percolator. At least a somewhat antique coffee maker, before they had electric ones. When I woke up I was given coffee ice cream. In the end the images associated with my tonsils did not make it onto the canvas. Other images, equally not truly remembered, found their way into the random pastiche. I can trace them to old photos and *bobbe-mayses* (folk tales) I was told. Some of the images I put in the panel were of objects I remember from years later but had been told they had been part of my life from the very beginning such as a pair of full size boxing gloves and a football placed in my crib before my arrival home from the hospital a couple days after I was born.

At one point my sister Judy reviewed my work. Judy had been an artist since the age of three when she would fall asleep in bed with crayons still in her hand. She had gone on for an MFA in painting. Life took some unexpected turns as she got pulled away from her painting and began raising a family. And then doctors discovered a brain tumor in her older son Ben at the age of 17. Ben finally succumbed at age 25. Toward the end of his life Ben told Judy that when he was gone she had to return to her artwork. This was part plea and part command from a young man who had become, through his courage, grace and immense sensitivity, a gentle teacher to those much older than he. He understood that her artwork would not only keep her alive but would be the way they would remain connected. So Judy did return to her art and unsurprisingly began to collect accolades and awards. In my mind Judy had always been the real artist in the family. I was a dabbler by comparison. So I gave great weight to her observations.

She told me the words I had incorporated into the painting didn't work where I had placed them. They distracted from the visual narrative. I also needed to work on creating a greater sense of spatial depth in the paintings, "to keep pushing it." Judy had actually spent some time with Wilhem de Kooning in his studio on Long Island in the late 60's and she was a great fan of his. "The great thing about space," he had said, "is that it keeps going."

I struggled with this idea because I saw my task as entirely different. I was not playing so much with space as I was with time. Of course, space was part of the visual equation. I wanted *Memory Calls* to reflect what I felt was the true nature of the relationship between memory and storytelling, between events as they actually happened and events as they were told. I wanted to demonstrate that what we think is a coherent narrative is really made up of, as Van Gogh suggested, "snatches of memory." I wanted to use a spatial art form to express ideas about time and memory. I really had no idea how to do this but I knew I had to resolve this dilemma between Judy's critique and what I felt was the essential role that words played in the overall project. I started to scrub out and paint over the words, but as a wink toward my decision I kept remnants of words on the canvas much like memories themselves are remnants of actual events. I have always believed that a painting should show the wounds and scars of battle.

But I resisted her suggestions related to space. I wanted the work to be closer in character to the Bayeux Tapestry with its flat, primitive quality than to a deeper sense of physical space and perspective. For me the essential element in the work related to a sense of the depth and the multi-layered dimensions of time. So I pushed a little, but not too much.

What Judy had suggested was to add a section of canvas at the bottom of the original canvas for the words. That would allow the visual images to stand more on their own terms on the upper portion. I liked the idea because then I could sew the pieces together and bring the character of the pieces closer to the Bayeux Tapestry. What bothered me though was the risk of then making it look like an annotated text. I felt stuck. And as was often the case when I was stuck I would place the canvas on the floor and walk around it. This gave me a way of looking at the piece from entirely different angles and sometimes this process yielded unexpected insights. Strangely enough, when I dropped the canvas to the floor it brushed against some photos I was using as a reference point. One photo landed under the canvas and the other—of my mother--nestled on top, skewed to the side.

I then began to circle the canvas without touching the photo. What struck me was the sense that the photo somehow belonged as part of the painting itself. The photo had actually been an integral part of the DNA of the process. In addition, I realized I not only wanted to capture the nature of memory but to leave evidence of the painting process as a way of showing that the act of painting and the act of remembering were parallel processes—both being forms of creative expression. So I thought that the photo needed to be part of the process. Incorporating the photo into the painting spoke to the accidental nature of the creative process. I thought that sometimes intentionality can straight-jacket a project and creativity required that the artist needed to be open to the accidents along the way and decide what to do with them. Simply because something is an accident doesn't mean it isn't useful or meaningful. In addition, the thought that had earlier come to me while reading Whitman's poetry returned: "Everything in." But that didn't settle the question of how to actually incorporate the photo. I did not want to incorporate the original photo. I couldn't bring myself to surrender it to the painting.

I had been aware of photo transfer techniques but had no idea how to do them. I pulled instructions off the internet and began to experiment. What I liked about the photo transfers was the ability to use images that created another layer of reality in the complex dance between truth, memory and illusion. The transfers gave the piece the sense of being anchored in a past reality. The transferred images made clear that the memories were not pure imaginings. Yet they enabled me to shape new imagery. The painting wasn't simply what you saw, it was a history of what you saw, an archeological evidence accumulated and tamped down over time by subsequent layers of remembered and burnished sediment.

I do not want to give the impression that I completed one canvas before going on to the next. I had taken 1942 pretty far before moving onto Meyer's Junk. However, I returned to 1942 many times to scrub, redo and add. In its final form each of the five canvases consists of two pieces. I completed the top part of each canvas before adding the bottom piece. I then clipped the bottom part of the canvas to the top part and began to work on it. I then took the top and bottom pieces to a tailor to sew them together. The tailor was a recent immigrant from Greece and his English was not very good. So I was pleased when he showed me the finished work. He proudly jabbed at the stitching, saying: "Two times. Very strong," as he tried to pull the pieces apart to show how fortified his handiwork was.

Every canvas is an experiment. And 1942 was my first experiment within the larger experiment of *Memory Calls*. I moved on to Meyer's Junk reluctantly without having resolved a number of issues. But I felt I needed to jump to the next experiment in part because I was interested to see how my efforts in Meyer's Junk might affect how I looked back at 1942. Matisse defined style as "the inability to do anything else." I think he meant that we each leave a recognizable signature on each piece of work that marks it as distinctly ours. That signature manifests itself from painting to painting or from one piece of work to another over time. We can trace that signature from the very beginning almost as though it is more artistic DNA than a freely chosen style. So I was curious to see how that "inability to do anything else" might show up in the other canvases.

While working on 1942 a friend visiting my studio ask me the following question: Does a painting flow from an idea or does an idea emerge from the painting? I think this is an important question because it applies to all creative projects whether a painting, a musical composition, a dance or creating within an altogether different realm such as creating a relationship or a business enterprise. It seems to me that if we are to move from the singular act of creativity to a state of creativeness we need to completely embrace the implications of how we respond to this question.

So let me begin by blowing up the question itself because I reject the either/or formulation out of hand.

The uneasy truth is that a painting, like any creative endeavor, comes to life not only through an iterative process, the give and take, sometimes beginning with an idea and other times the process itself yields ideas that come to contribute to or dominate the work. But if we were to scan the entire process from end to end much like an electrocardiogram we would see spikes on the graph representing certain episodes of heightened creative receptivity. These in fact would be the signs that creative agitation comes from the vast multiplicity of the modes of experience. A painting, like other kinds of creativity, can be triggered not only by a thought but also by an emotion or a physical sensation or a dream or by the profusion of the ways we experience life. Triggers are multi-sensory. And through the process, an idea, a sensation may also emerge which folds back on itself in a continuous loop of messy creativeness. The key is to remain open to these sources and to be able to spring off them in a way that contributes to the organic progression.

The lesson of 1942 and *Memory Calls* is that creativeness is fueled by the dynamic interplay between all the modes of experience.

Meyer's Junk

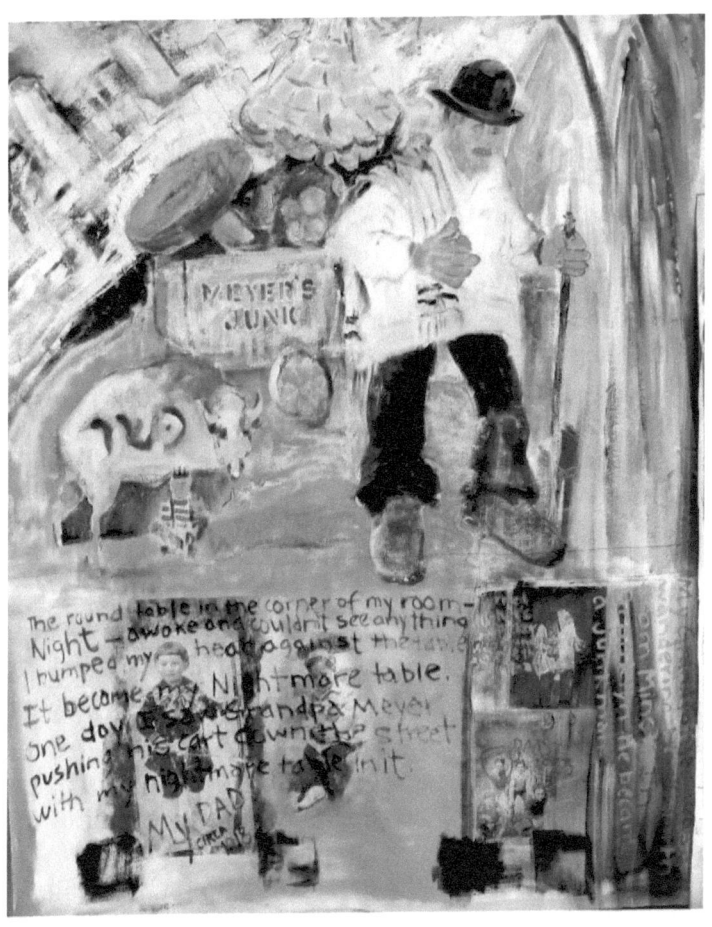

Meyer was my mom's father, my grandfather.

I have lots of visual images from the time we lived at 1551 East 33rd Street but they all strangely take place outdoors—with a single exception. I didn't like the dark. At night my parents would turn off the light in my bedroom and leave the door open a crack to allow the light from the rest of the apartment to seep into my room. I found this greatly comforting, not so much because I could make out the muted outlines of the things in my room but because I felt assured my parents were nearby.
I didn't have to worry about the dark chasm separating us or the fear that they might have been swallowed by it forever. One night when I was four or five years old I awoke to find the door to my bedroom had been shut tight and I could not see a thing. I got out of bed and, like a blind man, began groping for the door. I felt a terror roil up into my chest as I maneuvered for the door. After several steps my forehead knocked into a night table. I knew the table. It was made of mahogany and was round with little golden florets trimmed around its edge and an inlaid leather circle on top. I began to bawl and within an amount of time something less than forever my father swooped me up and had me on his lap. Eventually my sobbing subsided. It took several days for the swelling on my forehead to go away.

I came to call the table my nightmare table. I started running my hand over it before going to bed each night. This gave me great comfort. We became friends. I remember soon after that incident I let my parents close the door to my bedroom at night. I no longer needed the light to protect me from the dark chasm. My nightmare table stood watch. I can still feel its nubby top and smooth mahogany surface when I close my eyes.

Somewhere along the way my nightmare table and I got separated forever. I don't know what happened to it. A lamp sat on top of the table. The base was made of filigreed brass and its body was cloisonné in deep, rich green with large pink and white flowers. The lamp accompanied the family when we moved to Malverne when I was six years old. And after my parents died I took the lamp and still have it in my bedroom. I have no recollection of what happened to the nightmare table. I have had dreams of my Grandpa Meyer hauling the nightmare table and the lamp away in his junk cart.

Grandpa Meyer had been a blacksmith in Minsk. In America, he became a junkman. I remember feelings of embarrassment about that. I even have memories of seeing Grandpa Meyer pushing his cart up the street in Brooklyn and trying to hide so he wouldn't see me. I have no idea why I was embarrassed. I don't think I was old enough to understand the possible social stigma that went with such work. Perhaps I am overlaying feelings I had several years later. Grandpa Meyer was a short, stocky man always with a couple of days' stubble on his broad horse face. I recall him lifting me onto his lap while he took out a prayer book and jabbed at the brocaded Hebrew words with his calloused fingers as he tried to teach me the prayers. This was a hopeless endeavor because I mostly remember being overwhelmed by the odor of perspiration and schnapps on him.

It's hard to picture Grandpa Meyer bringing his young family through Ellis Island and out to the hills of Sioux City, Iowa where for six years he worked in his brother-in-law's broom factory before they came back east to Brooklyn. But that is where one of our family stories is embedded in mystery.

71

My mother was born in Sioux City and lived there for the first five years of her life.

When only a few months old, she was kidnapped by an Indian woman who lived on a nearby reservation. Along with the police Grandpa Meyer went to the reservation and recovered my mother. But years later a question began to surface within family lore. Did Grandpa Meyer return with the right baby? Was it really my mother? Had the Indian woman pulled a fast one? Am I half Jew and half Dakota Sioux? Grandpa Meyer and Grandma Dora denied such a possibility. *"Gornischt!* Enough! We don't know our own Hindaleh?" Of course it is highly unlikely that Grandpa returned with the wrong baby. But the question never seemed to go away.

Images of tents and the frontier have always played in my mind. I toyed with the possibility that they even ate kosher buffalo meat. But one of my favorite stories told how Buffalo Bill led a parade through the town in 1916. One of the mustangs broke loose and ran onto the front porch of my mother's house where my mom, in a carriage, and Aunt Tillie were watching the parade. None other than Buffalo Bill himself strode onto the porch, calmed the confused horse and saved my possibly Indian mother from near disaster.

These are true family stories.

Memory is tricky business. And so is the creative process. As I reflect on the whole enterprise of *Memory Calls*—how does one create a painting that contains images of the Brooklyn bridge, a tip of the hat to a French painter and a kosher buffalo? Only in America can such a work reflect reality.

In *Memory Calls* I found occasion to pay homage to certain painters I admired. When I came across

Manet's painting of The Ragpicker for the first time I was completely mesmerized. This encounter with the painting occurred many years ago, well before *Memory Calls* even came into my thoughts. But even then the painting evoked memories of my grandfather. I must have tucked the Manet image into a file folder somewhere in the back of my head. I have no idea how it reemerged into my awareness once I began to work on the piece. But there it was as vivid as Grandpa Meyer himself. So I used The Ragpicker as my model for painting Grandpa Meyer. I changed the rag slung over the Ragpicker's shoulder to a prayer shawl and I placed him at the foot of the Brooklyn Bridge rather than in Paris. Voila! Homage to a great artist. And to my Grandpa Meyer.

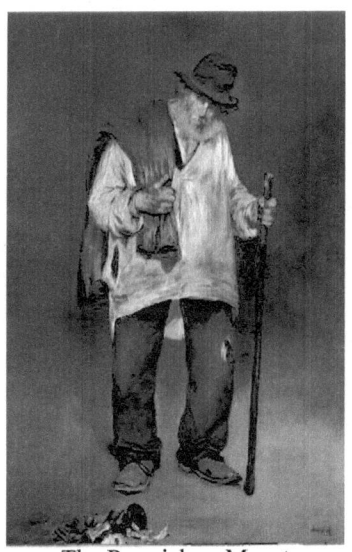

The Ragpicker, Manet

I felt so appreciative of The Ragpicker as the model for Grandpa Meyer that I decided to print a copy and use the photo transfer method to incorporate it into the painting. I thought the transfer showed an interesting juxtaposition between the original painting and my contemporized version in the form of Grandpa Meyer. As with other transfers I made a reverse image first and then slathered a thin layer of matt medium to secure it to the canvas. The following day I applied a wet rag to the paper and began rubbing it off with my fingers in a circular motion, taking great pleasure in watching the color image emerge underneath. As I surrendered to the rhythm of this process I noticed a thin red line of liquid squirting out of the paper and onto the canvas. At first I wondered whether I had not allowed some red paint to adequately dry before undertaking the transfer. But when I lifted my hand I noticed slivers of blood oozing from the tops of my fingers. I had rubbed the skin from my finger tips. And the blood had dried into the canvas.

I couldn't help but laugh at this. I had read a quote somewhere to the effect that writing is easy. You simply have to wait for the first drops of blood to fall on the page, then you begin. What I find funny about this idea is that we not only spill blood before creating a work of art, as an entry point into the creating act, but throughout the entire process of creating. If a work is going to be honest and not hide from itself or resort to artifice or take short cuts, the artist must pay the price. The price might not be actual blood but it is the emotional equivalent. I am not speaking here of revealing deep dark personal secrets on the canvas or page. And I am not one who advocates a martyr's view of an artist or the idea that an artist is a walking wound who feels pain more acutely than others. I am suggesting that making

74

meaningful art means pushing yourself beyond what you think you can do technically or even endure emotionally. It is important not to settle. That's where you begin to bleed—when you bump up against the skin of your efforts and sense that you need to go still further despite the belief you have no idea how to do so.

At one point in my sketchbook, frustrated by what I perceived as my own timidity, I wrote: "Nothing Protected, Everything Open." At the time, I was exhorting myself to let my guard down, to let go of inhibitions, even those I might not be aware of. I wrote those words almost as an acknowledgement that there were things inside me that were getting in the way. For me, the first half of that phrase was where the real challenge lay. This is where the blood begins dripping— when you prick the skin of emotional protectiveness that has grown around you over the years—and acknowledge your own vulnerability and be willing to push through it at the risk of not being good enough, at least according to your own standards. I think that's where the source of truth, art and surprise lives.

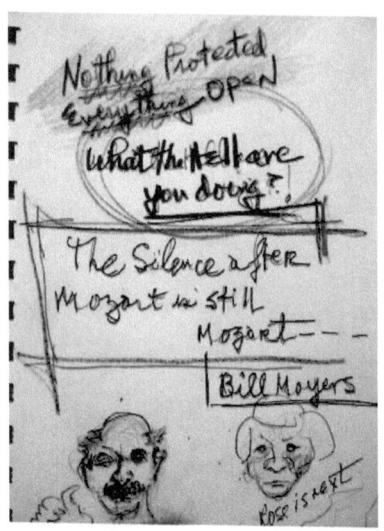

The real question then—aside from developing one's craft--is how does one do this? How does one allow "Nothing Protected" to become source rather than barrier?

How do I get myself into a state of Nothing Protected so I could let what was really inside me come out without filter, judgment, self-censure.

I believe there were two kinds of censure in play here. The first was self censure such as I just described. The kind of censure where you doubt that you have even the rudimentary talent to make art. But here I had an advantage. Call it obtuseness. I was obtuse enough to believe that even with limited talent, I could work hard to develop the talent side far enough to allow me to say what I wanted/needed to say. In other words, I was obtuse enough to believe that what I wanted to say was more powerful than my limited ability to say it and would therefore override any shortcomings of artistic talent. But the second kind of censure—social censure—was much

76

more bothersome. I actually didn't mind if someone said my painting was not very good. I knew I had much to learn and any inchoate efforts by their very nature must be bad. That is not to say they did not show promise, but they cannot by any measure be good. Nonetheless, this attitude did somewhat inure me against critiques about my talent. Rather, my sensitivity to social judgment was related to the very activity of painting itself—that others might view my engagement in art as frivolous, or quaint, or something one does after one has done something significant in one's profession. Art is a lovely adjunct, but hardly worthy of tenured status. My issue related more to identity. Could I claim to be an artist without experiencing that scraping sensation that comes with second guessing oneself?

Ultimately, I believe this was what I was exhorting myself to let go of. Nothing Protected, Everything Possible. I may not be good—yet—from a talent perspective. I may in fact never be good in that regard. But I am committed—I have something to say— by virtue of my declaration that I am an artist, if a fledgling one. There—I said it, I have nothing to lose. Nothing to protect. Lots of folks say artists are egotists. I really think it's just the opposite. If you are going to embark on the journey of becoming an artist you cannot have an ego. Or you need to be prepared to have yours crushed.

So where does memory end and imagination begin?

Tell me Grandpa Meyer—how much of you is real, how much remembered and how much imagined? This is what has come to me: A blacksmith from Nivyatza, Minsk Gubernia. One of 17 children. Wanderlust in your DNA. Not even the Czar's army could lasso you in. The photo on the wall of your apartment in Brooklyn shows you very stiff, constipated in your military uniform shortly before you accidently broke your sword while mounting a caisson. You are accused of treason against the Czar himself and brought to trial. Sentenced to death, you are put on a train and shipped off for execution. But you would have none of that. So you jumped off the train and grabbed Grandma Dora and Aunt Berry and Aunt Tillie and ran off to Poland, then England and, after a brief appearance at Ellis Island, made your way to Sioux City, Iowa, of all places for an observant Jew, where you went to work in a broom factory run by your brother-in-law. Even back then you would slip away for days—where?—on the vast hilly prairie of western Iowa—schnappsing it up with Buffalo Bill? Cavorting on the Indian reservation?—only to reappear, always before shabbos begins, slipping into your suit, vest and tie—shirt starched by Grandma Dora. And that one time, gone again for days in the middle of winter, no less, a vicious snow storm whiting everything out, the wind howling across the plain, snuffing out the fire in the stove so Grandma Dora wrapped Berry and Tillie and now also Jack and Hy and my mom Helen (Hindaleh) in thick clothes, blankets and bundled everyone into bed, snuggled together, shivering, waiting, as Grandma Dora later told us "for God to take us"— Jewish law prohibited lighting a fire on the Sabbath— when you burst into the house and, despite the fact that the sun had set and shabbos had arrived, you start a fire and saved the entire family.

Memory Calls and I wonder whose memory we are living? Is this memory made up? Is this memory actually memory or is it stories that have seeped into the heartwood of our family tree?

Does memory exist without imagination?

It seems to me that when an artist begins a particular work he is on only one leg of a larger journey. This larger journey is a lifetime quest for mastery, meaning and self. Yet we are meagerly equipped when we begin. I draw comfort from others. Gautier-Brzeska did not have a fully equipped sculptor's studio in the trenches during WWI. In fact, he only had his bayonet and the butt of a mauser. His most important equipment rested deep within him and it was with those resources he carved something "gentler" to his soul. Who knows where his longer journey would have taken him had he survived and what he could have revealed to us along the way. So each individual work is a single letter in a longer word, longer sentence, paragraph, chapter, story, sometimes quietly composed, most often unnoticed by the world at large. For many of us this is a lonely journey, likely unrecognized, with a limited audience.

Ultimately we create because of these things inside us. They have no name. It is the very absence of a name that gives them such power. They are sourced deep, deep within us. The best we can do is assign them to the realm of the mysterious. Their dumb power believes that somewhere someone will see, hear, read and our signs and voices will echo beyond the grave.

I think of Grandpa Meyer as an artist. True, he was a blacksmith in Russia, turned junkman in Brooklyn. It wasn't the scraps of junk pulled from peoples' discards that he turned like alchemy into a meager handful of coin that made him an artist. It wasn't the craftsman's hand and unyielding anvil that turned metal into horseshoes and iron door latches. But it was these things without name that he shaped into the will to survive and give life to a family in a strange land. Others had sentenced him to death. Others had composed the paragraph describing his execution but before the last could be finished he grabbed the pen with his iron-blackened hand and wrote his own narrative. It was something deep within that gave such power to this act of creation and it was the same power that compelled his calloused finger to jab at the page of brocaded Hebrew hieroglyphics in order to pass these things with no name on to his frightened grandson.

After we had moved to Long Island we celebrated Grandpa Meyer's 75th birthday at our house in Malverne. We had a birthday cake covered in blue and white icing and all the aunts, uncles, and cousins came out to present him with a gold Movado wrist watch. He sat in a chair around the dining room table, his perfect false teeth flashing joy and embarrassment at his extended brood. As proud as he was, he looked uncomfortable sitting in one place for so long. His restless spirit needed to stretch its legs so after cutting the cake he said he had to go to the bathroom and while we waited for his return he slipped out the side door and disappeared into the extended maze of flat suburban streets. After a while we figured he had gone AWOL and the aunts and uncles vigorously debated whether they should go after him or let him do his thing. Wisdom prevailed and as the summer dusk began to fade Grandpa Meyer reappeared through the same side door from which he had gone in pursuit of some inexplicable compulsion to wander—he returned as he always had, as though nothing had happened.

Several months later we received a phone call that Grandpa Meyer had been mugged on Chester Street where he lived and the watch stolen. He had put up a fight and received a swollen cheek and eye for his efforts. According to an eye witness he had gotten up after being knocked to the ground and shook his fist at the perpetrators, yelling *"Mayn kinder, mayn kinder!"* It wasn't the watch he cried after. "My children! My children!" he lamented. The thieves had stolen his children.

My sister Judy tells the story of walking to Lindner Place Elementary School one day in the fifth grade. In order to get there she had to walk by the railroad station at the center of town. On this particular day, though, she was completely taken by surprise when Grandpa Meyer stepped out of the last car of an outbound train and looked around as though he was not certain which direction he wanted to go. And he did not appear surprised to see his young granddaughter standing right in front of him as though he had ordered her up ahead of time.

When Judy asked him what he was doing here, he said he felt like visiting Helen, my mom. Judy asked if Mom was expecting him and he simply said "Expect me? Why?" Perhaps he had slipped out the back door of his apartment on Chester Street, like he had done from the side door of our house on his birthday, to heed the wandering call. Perhaps he thought of paying an unexpected visit to his daughter Helen only after he had begun to weave his way through the streets of Brooklyn because he needed to be headed somewhere. I have no idea how he figured out how to get to the Long Island Railroad and pinch out the change for a ticket to Malverne. And I have no idea how he expected to find our house since he had never done this before and could not have known how to get from the station to the house. Perhaps he thought he only needed to ask any passerby where Helen lived and he would be directed to her doorstep and that she would be home. I always marveled at how the road always seemed to lead Grandpa Meyer where he wanted to go. Many years later, during a period of heavy business travel I remember saying to Karen and the kids that no matter where I am traveling I feel like I am always on the way home. Only now do I realize I must have been channeling Grandpa Meyer.

The Illusion of Free Will

At what point do you recognize that you have ceded control of a work? At some point you have put in motion a series of choices freely made, without encumbrances except for the ones you are unaware of—and those may be substantial—so that you have an illusion of free will. After all, you are the creator. You choose the ground, the palette, the style of representation, the design, and on and on. At some point, though, a little invisible genie enters your consciousness—I think it is the emerging voice of the work you are trying to create. It asserts its influence. It does not allow you to do this or that. You are aware that this invisible gnome is imposing limitations on your choices. At some point it actually grabs the brush from your hand, lays out your paints on the palette. You hear its voice whispering "that will not do," "push more in this direction." You are no longer free because the work itself has taken on a character that will not allow you to stray wildly away. Yes, you can improvise within limits. You can push the envelope but not tear it. You become captive of your own work and your role is simply to enable it, to serve it.

The Grandmas

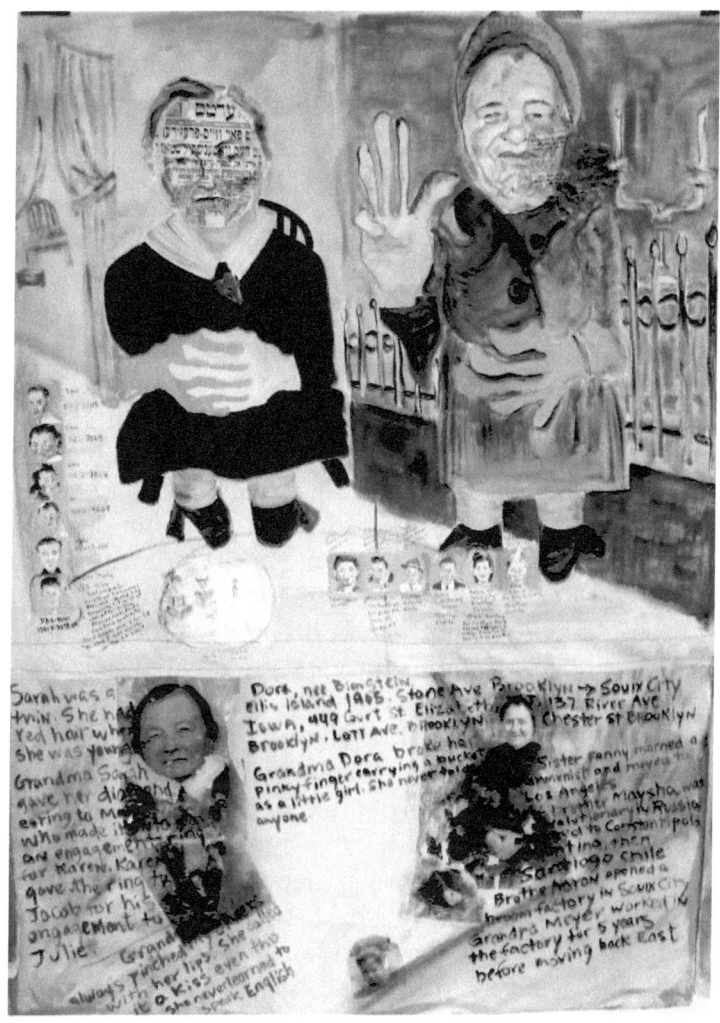

I remember waking up the morning I was to begin a new panel, and that put me in an agitated state. In many ways, every canvas is a new beginning. In some ways your options are infinite. But I had established a commitment to a kind of primitive look per the Bayeux Tapestry. Nonetheless I had not gotten any further in my thoughts than painting each of my grandmothers onto the canvas. Despite having made many sketches in my sketchbook of Grandma Sarah and Grandma Dora I had no idea what else would emerge on the canvas. I had no grand scheme or design in mind.

I had gotten into the habit of leafing through the old family album during breaks. By immersing myself in the images of an earlier time and place I could often coax myself into a state of gentle melancholy, of longing for the magical ability to slip back in time to that past reality. In some sense it was a way of priming the pump. In fact, I found that the photos brought me back into parts of the rooms and streets that had never made it into the frame of the camera lens. If the camera had missed them, not so memory. I became a time traveler walking into the nooks and crannies of Grandma Dora's kitchen or opening her galvanized metal bread basket perched precariously on the outside window sill. I took in the thick aroma of *fleischke* (meat) beet borscht, the sweet doughy smell of baking challah. Grandma Sarah's sitting room filled with a strange combination of a sap green, velveteen chair and ottoman and bumpy couch. Tasseled, pomegranate colored curtains rose in back of the couch. A copy of *The Daily Jewish Forward* in Yiddish on the ottoman. Poor as church mice they were—a tailor and housewife--but to me this was a home befitting a sultan. I could close my eyes and feel the tailor's hands lift me to his lap and marvel at the hard sucking candy Grandpa Harry magically pulled from my ear.

My mom's mom, Grandma Dora, was a strong woman so I knew how I wanted to paint her. Standing erect in her overcoat—the photo I used as a reference point was black and white but I remembered the coat being green—her matching babushka wound around her head. Her right hand held up so the world could finally see her pinky finger broken as a little girl and hidden from her parents until it healed permanently bent against her palm. She never mentioned why she was too frightened to tell her parents about her finger. In truth, I can't imagine Grandma Dora as a young girl. I think she was old from the beginning.

In many ways, one of the most important decisions a painter makes is what not to put into a painting. In reality, the eye is indiscriminate. It takes it all in. But art is a discerning craft. Otherwise there is no distinction between art and the physical act of seeing. Life drafts, art edits. So art gives grace to the language of seeing by picking and choosing, by arranging relationships of images, colors, tones. Even given my predilection to take an "everything in" approach for *Memory Calls* based upon my belief that such an approach comes closest to capturing the nature and experience of memory—even given this predilection, I found myself needing to trim down what I let into The Grandmas painting. To me, their lives had been so epic, spanning continents, years and events that I wanted them to stand on their own, testaments to endurance and their singularity. I thought I only needed one or two items to act as flying buttresses to the architecture of their identity. And here is where mystery enters. I painted the candelabra I remembered from Grandma Dora's apartment. She was a fiercely devout Jew. But then I was stumped. I did not know what else, if anything else, to add. So I went on to another part of the painting. But an image of a wrought iron fence kept coming into my head. It seemed to be a particular fence with spade shaped tops. I couldn't call it a memory. It was more like a flashing image. Several nights later I had a dream in which Grandma Dora brought me as a little boy to her shul. I didn't want to go. I didn't feel comfortable among the old men with prayer shawls draped over their heads, furiously bobbing up and down, their mumbled voices rising in cacophonous waves of prayer. As she pulled me along we passed through a large wrought iron fence—the very one that kept showing up in my head—which rose higher and higher until, once within its boundaries, it closed behind us.

The next day I painted the fence onto the canvas—first as imagined, then as dreamed. Then something strange happened. I had an old post card sent by the rabbi of my grandparents' old synagogue. The post card was an announcement of some event at the synagogue and had the name of the synagogue and its address on it. Soon after painting the fence onto the canvas, I came across a book on the internet titled *The Lost Synagogues of Brooklyn.* I ordered the book. And when it arrived I quickly opened it and found not only the name of the synagogue but a current photo. The old brick synagogue is now The Peoples Baptist Church. The current owners of the building have left the cornice with a Star of David above the main entrance (I painted this cornice into The Grandpas canvas) and the name in Hebrew: Ahavath Achim Anshei. In front of the church is a wrought iron fence. Almost exactly as I had painted it in my painting! How does this happen? Did the creative process set the table for the image of the fence to arise? Did remembering different things trigger the memory of the fence? What else is in the memory bank that we are not conscious of? What conditions enable us to lure them back to consciousness? Was painting the fence actually a conscious choice I made or was something else guiding me, compelling me to place it in evidence?

Time is warped to the contours of memory. We may recall an event or series of events, but they seem to compress into dense stars whose gravitational pull will not let us go. Passover seders are such a star. There were many of them—sometimes at Grandma Sarah's and Grandpa Harry's apartment, sometimes up in Utica New York at Aunt Tillie's two family house, sometimes at our place—they blend into one extended memory—thick with smells and chatter, some in Yiddish, singing prayers, drinking cups of Manishewitz Concord wine, Elijah, the afikomen and tears. They survive as photographs, washed out and frozen, but in my mind they burst with energy and remembering. The singing, thumping on the table, praying seem to drone on forever. Then the parsley and salt water, then the eggs in salt water and the bitter herbs and Hillel sandwich, the gefilte fish and then finally the rich, ruby red *fleishke* (meat) beet borsht—steaming, filled with grated beets, juicy morsels of flanken beef and the sweet broth. Then the afikomen—the slice of matzah without which you cannot complete the seder—hidden by a grownup, discovered by one of us kids and returned in exchange for a shiny silver dollar. Then the thumping begins again with the *birkat hamazon*—the prayer after the meal. It goes on and on and they are pointing their fingers at me. I am 5 years old. Look, little Freddie's drunk! I put my head down on the table. Then I sink under the table and begin to cry. A feeling of humiliation grabs a hold and I can't stop crying until it is replaced by long, deep, dry shuttering breathing. No hand reaches under the table. No words are spoken. Above me the prayers and thumping inexorably move to their conclusion. A hand reaches under the table. But I do not recognize it. I am fast asleep. I hated Passover and now I love it, even the memory of my humiliation. Passover does not show up in *Memory Calls*. But the love is in every brush stroke. The unseen in the seen.

Moving to Malverne opened a whole new world to me. Utterby Road seemed to be on the edge of a frontier. Immediately next to our house was a farm, and in the summer tall stalks of corn rose like green sky scrapers beckoning me to get lost within its canyons. On the other side of the farm you could cross a road that led into a deep forest filled with damp mossy trees and streams leading to a large pond where you could spy on large white swans. Across the street from our house was a reedy swamp where you could hunt for frogs and snakes. In the summer fireflies as lively as sparklers lit the night sky. Brooklyn was crowded and the buildings rubbed up against each other and you could hear neighbors through the walls of the apartment buildings and across the alleys. But Long Island teemed with a different kind of life. Over the years I watched as the swamp across the street turned into curving streets with small brick houses and the forest across the street turned into open fields for a new high school.

I met my first friend riding a tricycle a couple of houses down from me. Hank and I became fast friends. Mi casa es su casa. My mom had brought all the Jewish traditions out to the Island. She and my dad helped establish the first synagogue in Malverne, and my Dad built the first arch which housed the synagogue's torah scrolls. Mom worked hard to make every holiday special. She would put on plays every Purim and we would play the roles of Haman, Esther and Mordecai. Then she served homemade humantashin. At Passover we would search the house with a feather looking for chumetz crumbs and change the dishes and pots and pans. At Chanuka she always made lots of latkes and apple sauce colored with blue or red food dye.

Hank also came from a Jewish family but they belonged to a Reform temple. This meant they adhered less to the traditional observances. They even had a Christmas tree at Chanuka. This was the first time I had ever seen a Christmas tree in person. To me this seemed so alien. But I was mesmerized by the tinsel and trinkets with which they adorned the tree and the bounty of presents—wrapped in Chanuka paper—tucked under the tree. When I got home that afternoon I found only Grandma Dora there. I told her I wanted a Christmas tree, believing that was the normal thing for Jews on Long Island to do. I will never forget the look on her face. Her features immediately contorted into an expression of profound and mortal shock, confusion and fear. She cupped her hands to her chest as though her heart were about to spill out. Then she grabbed my shoulders and shoved me back out the door into the snowy dusk. *"Aroise! Aroise foon hoise!"* she shouted. Out, get out of the house right now!

I think Grandma Dora always looked at me as damaged goods from that day forward and Malverne as the threshold of *gehenem* (hell) itself.

And perhaps she was right. One summer night when I was 19 years old I woke from a sleep dripping in sweat. We were living in Malverne and Grandma Dora was living with us. We kept a kosher home. Separate dishes, silverware. We only brought kosher meat into the house. We even had a rabbi come to the house and assure Dora that we maintained an entirely compliant kosher home. But Malverne was not Brooklyn. And a kosher home in Malverne was really not kosher as far as Grandma Dora was concerned. So she had her own pots and pans and dishes and silverware. She would prepare her own meals. Truth be told, we did not keep kosher outside the house. By then our souls had been entirely corrupted despite the fact that our home was kosher and we regularly went to synagogue and my mom was president of Hadassah and the sisterhood and I had had a bar mitzvah. Nonetheless, on many Sunday evenings we would go out for Chinese food and order shrimp rolls or lobster Cantonese.

Earlier that day I had gone to Manhattan Beach in Brooklyn to play basketball. Manhattan Beach was a basketball Mecca. Ballplayers from all over the New York City area came to show their stuff. You played games of three on three, half court, and you stayed on the court until another team beat you. I went there with Artie Heyman, who was to become the college player of the year at Duke the next year and eventually be drafted by the New York Knicks, and with Normie Goldsmith, who played at Syracuse and had earlier been voted the nation's top high school player of the year by Parade Magazine. We ran the table at 10 straight games without losing and then went to Lundy's, the legendary seafood restaurant in Sheepshead Bay. I ordered one of their large shrimp cocktails to go but couldn't finish it on the drive back to the island. By the time I got home it was late and everyone was in bed so I put the container of shrimp in the fridge. When I woke drenched in sweat hours later I realized I had committed a mortal sin. If Grandma Dora ever discovered the carton of shrimp she would have left the house in the middle of the night, never to return, never to speak to my mother again. The family would be torn asunder by my act of thoughtlessness. Not wanting to lose a second I ran downstairs in my briefs and bare feet and pulled the carton of shrimp from the refrigerator. I ran outside and dumped the carton into a garbage can.

In graduate school I made an abrupt turn. It was in the midst of my mom and dad's illnesses and for reasons I do not fully understand I decided I would keep kosher. I am not sure whose voices had been speaking to me. There were so many of them. I have never wavered from that decision even now as the voices grow ever more muffled.

We are lost and found many times in our lives. Perhaps I keep a kosher home as an act of repentance. Perhaps as a grasping for continuity and connection. Perhaps for reasons that do not make sense—not as an extension of logic, or faith, or tradition, but as an act of love. There Grandma Dora is on the canvas—solid, erect, anchored by the wrought iron fence, emblematic of her faith, ancient as the tales in the Old Testament, painted there by her wayward grandson. Can art be a form of prayer? An act of supplication? A cry for redemption? For Forgiveness? Love the Lord your God with all your heart, with all your soul, with all your might. And these words which I command you this day shall be in your heart. Can you have tradition in the absence of belief? How do love, redemption, the cry for forgiveness show up in a painting? Perhaps they do not. Perhaps they cannot. But perhaps they do. The unseen in the seen. There is no art without the unseen.

My dad's mom, Grandma Sarah, presented another challenge altogether. She was a mystery to me. She barely spoke English and her Yiddish, like a bird chirping, was just as indecipherable. I was told she was a twin. Her tightly bound grayish bun hid any traces of her youthful red hair. We could barely talk to each other. Her English was almost nonexistent and my Yiddish even more so. What tales did I miss? What stories are lost about the rushed escape from Poland? Her family? She cupped my chin and cheeks in the palms of her hands and stared into my eyes, bobbing her head from side to side as though in prayer, saying *"oy, mein kind, shana punim, shana punim."* My child, such a beautiful face, such a beautiful face. And then she pinched her tightened lips on my cheek in a kiss that felt more like a bite.

I am painting the portrait of Grandma Sarah, her smallness, her quiet, and I feel her opaqueness. I wonder what she was really like. I know her least. Months later I am looking at her image and I recall copies of *The Jewish Daily Forward* in Yiddish on the ottoman or spread out on the kitchen table in its indecipherable Yiddish letters—as though they formed an inscrutable mask over her face. I tracked down YIVO to see if they had an archive of old copies of the newspaper. They put me in touch with the Museum of Jewish History in New York and I requested old copies of The Forward dating back to 1905 when Grandpa Meyer and Grandma Dora first immigrated here and then 1910 when Grandpa Harry and Grandma Sarah came. I cut out a mask from the copies and transferred the print onto her face.

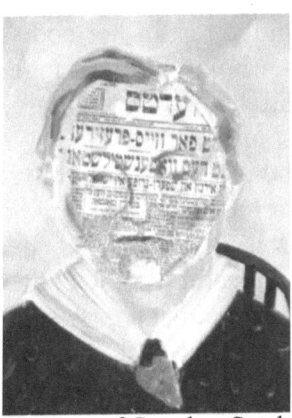
Close-up of Grandma Sarah

Dominoes. I have images of her and Grandpa Harry sitting at their dining room table, domino tablets spread randomly before them, she, lifting one from the pile and gently placing it alongside another, exhaling as though she had just rescued a nestling from a predator. She tilted her head toward Grandpa Harry with a look that suggested triumph and a request for forgiveness at the same time. She was a gentle, quiet soul beloved by her six children, my father the youngest of them. I remember a cardboard panel taped to the wall next to her telephone. On the panel, from oldest to youngest, were photos of each of her children and next to each photo were their telephone numbers. She could not read their names in English. So the children improvised and put the photos rather than their names there. I felt compelled to find the actual telephone numbers that had sat on the cardboard panel. So I tracked them down through old microfiche at the Brooklyn Library and recovered them for the painting.

I painted Grandma Sarah sitting in a chair, like a queen. Her hands folded neatly on her lap. Her right wrist severed from the rest of her body—a sense that she could not be fully whole in this strange land of America. And another chair, behind the curtain, unoccupied, the mystery of the rest of her.

There is the question of the mystery of the rest of us in all of us. I remember Grandma Sarah, rescuing the domino tablet from the jumbled pile and giving it momentary meaning and order by connecting it to a sister tablet, a fellow traveler, just so. A small gesture. I keep telling myself that each brush stroke is like a domino tablet connecting itself to what went before, a striving for wholeness.

Bearing Witness

I cannot help but believe art is a form of bearing witness. The artist's eye is uniquely suited for this role because it tunes into experience at so many levels—the observed, the imagined, the unseen, the felt—and recapitulates that experience into new forms that outlive the experience itself, that give it a kind of immortality. In many ways the world of 17th century Delft is lost to us but how vividly we see life's drama played out in the two rooms of Vermeer's paintings. These particular rooms at this particular time in this particular geography become a world stage on which loss, mystery, libido, greed, grace, justice, redemption are captured and conveyed in stunning, breathtaking beauty. Goethe once suggested that if we were to find the universal then we must pursue the particular in every direction. By bearing witness to the particular, art gifts us insights into the universal human condition.

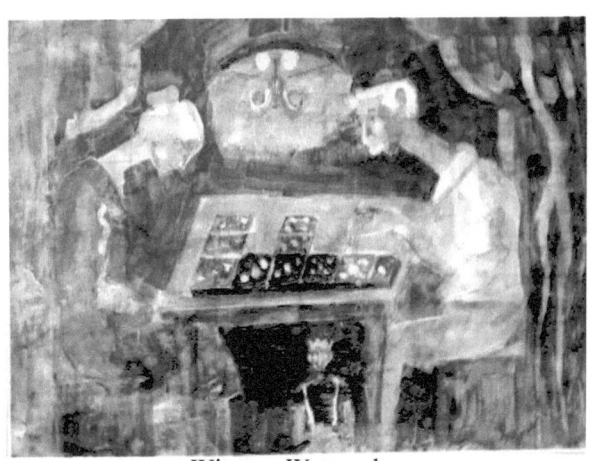
Witness, Watercolor

    I felt it was important that the idea of bearing witness show up in *Memory Calls*. In an earlier watercolor I made of Grandma Sarah and Grandpa Harry playing dominoes I had placed an image of myself under the table—an unseen observer—a witness. In this painting I wear a cap I had noticed in an earlier photo of me while living on East 33rd Street. So I decided to adopt this image of myself—pointed cap, polo shirt and suspenders—in each of the paintings. I am a witness in all the scenes, even when I could not have been present, except in my imagination. In that sense we are witnesses to the world our imaginations create. In fact, I incorporated this image of me into the 1942 painting so I am entering the world as a witness even though at the time all I could do was scream out in dismay at the cold, bracing reality of the world.

The Grandpas

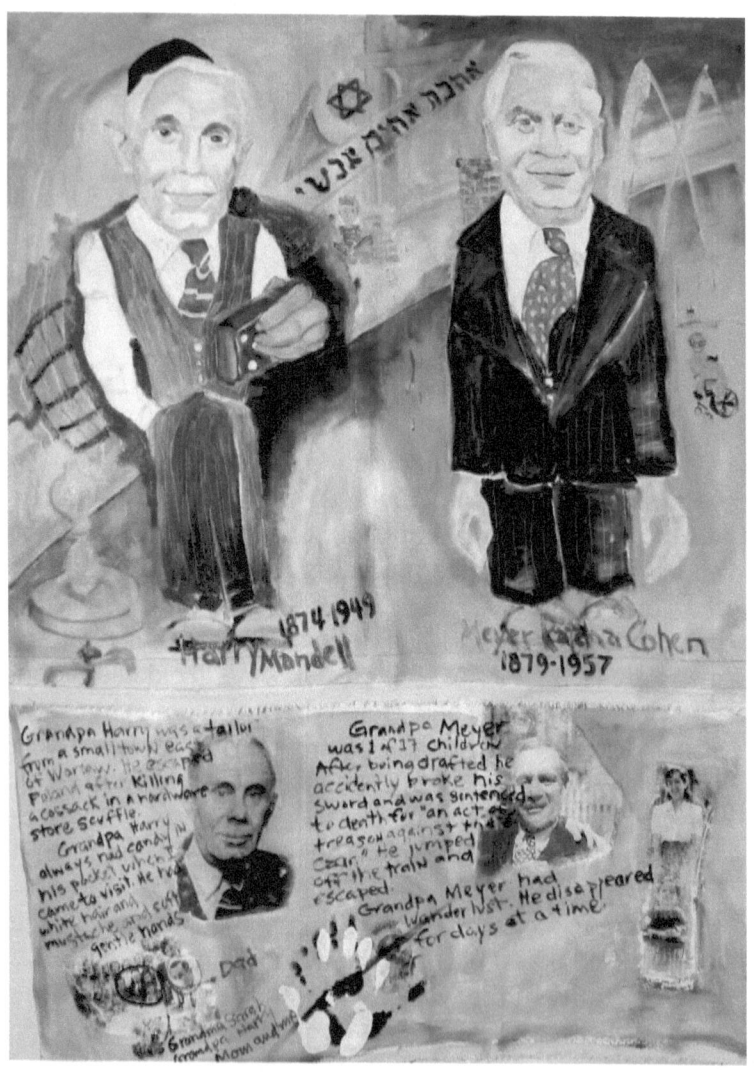

96

When is a painting finished? Rembrandt suggested that a painting is finished when an artist has achieved his aims in it. De Kooning said he knew a painting was finished when he painted himself out of it. I am not sure what that means or what that looks like. I really don't have a satisfactory answer for myself. I have often thought a painting was finished and even hung it on the wall only to discover places where I could express things differently. In fact, I am still tinkering with *Memory Calls* even as I am writing about it as a finished work. Karen often scolds me for not signing my pieces. Good enough for the wall but not for your signature? But the wall is simply another form of scrutiny, another perspective. The wall reveals what the easel cannot. A surrogate form of letting go. Not really yet letting go. A test run but not too late to be reclaimed by the easel. The dilemma is that perfection cannot come from imperfection. We are imperfect beings and we cannot help but reflect that imperfection in our work. To compound matters we are continuously evolving in our imperfection. The truth is we view even our own work through a moving lens. In some sense a painting is truly done only when the artist is dead, when his natural meddling impulses are also put to rest.

So one of the challenges an artist faces is to learn to let go. At some point the issue becomes less about when the work is finished than what you are not creating by continuing to work on an imperfect piece. This of course begs other questions. Are you hanging on because you wish to avoid the terror of starting a new piece? Are you holding on because you fear the judgments that might befall the piece if you say, in fact, it is finished? This sensitivity is heightened by the fact that artists who truly express themselves, as opposed to those who play with artifice, are vulnerable because the form and content of expression is revelatory. It amounts to putting one's emotional entrails on the table.

These questions were very much in play as I worked on The Grandpas canvas. On a visual level this canvas is the sparsest of the five that make up *Memory Calls*. But it is emotionally quite dense. For me, the question of when this piece was finished became clear in a most unexpected way—when I was able to experience the actual smells I associated with Grandpa Harry and Grandpa Meyer. I did not start out with this as my aim. And the phenomenon came as quite a surprise. But it was as real and alive as if Grandpa Harry and Grandpa Meyer were fully breathing and standing right in front of me.

Even more surprising were the variety of smells and fragrances. Starched shirts and the sweet fragrance of sucking candy. Sponge cake and the faint hint of moth balls. The steamy aroma of a freshly pressed suit. Grandpa Harry always smelled clean. Grandpa Meyer's odors rose from the canvas more full bodied and earthy. His fishy breath co-mingled with the fermented bouquet of perspiration and schnapps.

This was my world, the world I moved about in every day, but it was strange at the same time. It was a world in which I was never comfortable. I was inhabitant and outsider at the same time.

In The Grandpas canvas the walls of the synagogue are crumbling. That world is gone. I sit among a pile of bricks, witness to that world, yet too young to understand it. It is only now that I love that world, love what I can no longer experience. I sometimes think that art is a kind of communion between the artist and the subject. An act of consummate empathy.

Ultimately, art is a refusal to be anything less than here. Now. Even when the subject is then. What ultimately gets created is mediated by this empathy felt in the here and now and is transformed into something no longer gone but new.

I later found out that my dad's father, Grandpa Harry, was a murderer and my mom's father, Grandpa Meyer, a fugitive from Russian justice after being sentenced to death for affronting the Czar. Give me your tired, your poor, your huddled masses yearning to breathe free. Yes, and your murderers and criminals.

As the family tells it, Grandpa Harry was waiting in line at a hardware store in his town in Poland when a Cossack entered, jumped to the front of the line and starting shouting something about "the Jews." A scuffle followed. Harry got into a shoving match and the Cossack stumbled backward, fell and hit his head on a shovel and died. This from the gentlest soul I ever met. As the family story goes Harry grabbed Sarah and children Danny and Fay and Ida (no one seems to know how long this took. Hours? Days? Weeks?) and fled on a boat to Ellis Island. Over the years I tried to get more details about the events surrounding Grandpa Harry's murderous act and narrow escape only to be told the story almost exactly as I have told it here. With no more nor less detail. Grandpa Harry died when I was six years old. I did not know him well but what I did know made my imagination happy. Years later my dad said that the only things Grandpa Harry left behind besides the furniture in his apartment and the clothes on his back was a pocket full of charity stubs. I never knew they had been there, those charity stubs, as he always pulled a handful of hard sucking candies from that same pocket whenever I visited. His English was not that good, but I always felt comforted standing near him or sitting on his lap. And his white moustache never really tickled when he burrowed his face into my neck and whispered in mixed English and Yiddish: *"a bisl* a tickle for Feivel." A little tickle for Feivel. Feivel was my Yiddish name and he was the only one who used it.

Grandpa Meyer was different.

"Leyenden! Leyenen!" Grandpa said to me, poking his finger at the prayer book. "Read! Read!" He held me on his lap, his tangy breath pushing out the Yiddish commands. Had I known then what I came to learn I might have tried harder to decipher the Hebrew words rather than squirm in rebellion. He was a Jew in the Czar's army. Conscripted, he accidentally broke his sword, a punishable act. Tried for treason against the Czar. Convicted and sentenced to death. He jumped off the train to escape and, with Grandma Dora and daughters Berry and Tillie, made his way through Ellis Island to Sioux City, Iowa.

"Gehnook! Gornisht mit gornisht!" "Enough. Nothing with nothing," he says to me and shrugs his shoulders.

"To you this is nothing?" He points to me. "Yes, *gornisht mit gornisht.* It is life. My life," he says, "I jumped off the train and came to America. *Nu?* So?

That America is gone. The synagogue in Brooklyn is now a Peoples' Baptist Church, the bricks crumbling, the cornice teetering on its side."

Grandpa, Grandpa, your refrain echoes in my ear. *Gornisht mit gornisht.* Nothing with nothing. You jumped off the train and came to America! So?

This is your story, Grandpa. Now it is my memory.

100

And yet, some part of me feels like I've betrayed you and your world. Of the few things you carried from Minsk, one was a hand-embroidered, black felt yarmulke. I remember the glow of affection in my mother's eyes when you gently laid it on my head in your apartment on Chester Street. You sat on a wooden chair in the dining room that also served as the living room and the extra bedroom. You ceremoniously lifted the yarmulke from the metal topped dining table. The silver-plated Shabbat candelabra, high on the cupboard, looked over us. I stood between your knees. You recited the blessing for a son: "May God give you the blessings of Ephraim and Menasseh." A gift. My birthright. But I treated it as though it were infected with leprosy.

To the five-year-old, it was an extension of your gruff, smelly, over powering presence. You smacked of strangeness and threat. Your coming to live with us was an intrusion into my comfortable world. A tear in the soft fabric of my inner world. I always felt like squirming away from you. My moment came when we moved from Brooklyn to Malverne, miles away on Long Island. I wrapped the yarmulke in a brown paper bag and buried it in the backyard. And then I tried to forget it. I tried for months and months. And then a year. But I was like a little Raskolnikov, torn apart inside by my crime, my deceit.

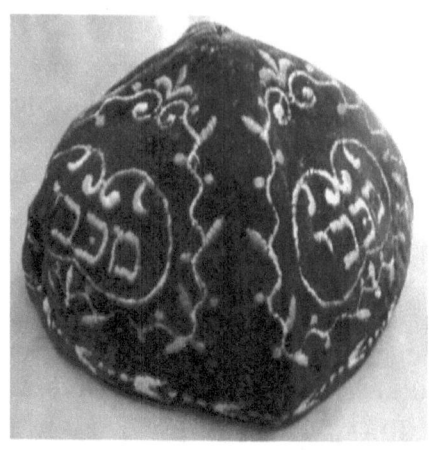

One day, Mom asked for the yarmulke. I pretended to have lost it. She went on a silent, desperate search around the house. She was cross with me for losing it. I felt a momentary reprieve. Lost was not so bad. If she knew what I had really done! Then one night, unable to withstand my guilt any longer, I took a flashlight and dug it up, relieved that it had not been eaten by worms after more than a year in the soft, moist earth. I told my mom I had found it. At first, I wanted her to see me as a hero. But something in my seven year-old's psyche knew that such a wish was a compounding of sins. I burst into tears and threw myself at her, confessing through sobs every cowardly detail of my crime. She held me until my crying subsided. She did not speak.

Even then I expected her recriminations. I knew my tears would not absolve me of my deceit. I steeled myself for her admonishments, for the anticipated look of profound disappointment in her eyes.

"You are a good boy," she said softly. "It took courage to tell me the truth."

Through the blurriness of my tears I searched her eyes. I was looking for a hint of censure, a suggestion of recrimination. I searched and searched. Could she truly not hold some measure of judgment against her son's act of betrayal? But I could not find any of it. She simply put her lips to the top of my head.

Only my mother could transform betrayal into an act of courage. Fear and trembling into love. She was speaking to the best in me, even though I could not recognize it myself.

"BIG"

It was not unusual for me to bring my one and half year old grandson Baylor into my studio during the time I was working on *Memory Calls*. My thought was to have him leave a mark on one of the canvases. From great great grandson to great great grandfather. One day Baylor comes down to my studio and picks up a "Big." A "Big" is a small fleck of dust he notices on the floor. That's what he calls it. In his soft, bewildered voice. To me a "Big" barely warrants attention. "Bigs" are part of the messiness of things. But Baylor has a different take on "Big." These miniscule dust balls are of great significance to Baylor. He found them disturbing. But there was something else about how he took such great joy mixed with a touch of nervousness in finding a "Big." It was as though he and he alone had discovered something others had missed. Even the smallest fleck of dust needed to be shown respect—indifference would not do--even if that respect meant the "Big" was to be done away with. A "Big" needed its moment of recognition.

103

So he remained ever vigilant and when he noticed one he lifted the dust ball toward me and pinched it between his forefinger and thumb and ever so quietly whispered "Big." Meaning, Behold, here is a Big, what a marvel others have missed. And now we need to remove this.

I sometimes feel like an undiscovered BIG. A fleck of dust in the great scheme of things. Why do I bother to paint when I do not believe my work will ever be recognized?

A child's eyes are not our eyes. They remind us that even a speck of dust has significance, cannot go unnoticed. This speck of dust must be told "I see you. You cannot be ignored." In this moment I recognize you as being in the world. Whatever the future may hold, in this moment, I acknowledge you. Baylor gives me hope that my work may one day be given a moment of consideration before it disappears into the greater indifference of the universe. I paint so that somewhere at some time someone with child's eyes will encounter my work, perhaps be touched by it, and pronounce the word "BIG".

"Enchanted by Snatches of the Past"

Memory is like looking at stones through the surface of a stream. The stones look closer than they really are. They appear fuzzy and wobbly. The movement of the water's dancing surface blurs their outline. The actual stones are different than our experience of them through the water's surface. Yet, the water's version is no less real. Different and real. I think this is the case with memory. What we remember is not the original thing. It is a version seen through the watery lens of time. But it is its own reality. The irony is that we construct our stories around these memories and even though these stories are built on the imperfection of our recollections they become their own new truth. We become, as Van Gogh writes, enchanted by snatches of the past. They take hold of our imagination and we surrender to their power.

It occurred to me that the paintings of my grandparents were representations of photographs that were themselves representations of my grandparents. The paintings were several times removed from the real people and the real events. Neither the paintings nor the photographs replicated the direct experience I had had of them. Both my memory and the paintings fell short in significant ways. The truth is that it couldn't be any other way. But it made me sad to acknowledge that I was possibly creating another layer of deception.

I really didn't see any way around this.

No matter what I did from a creative perspective the past reality was the past reality and the present reality was a completely different thing. So rather than fool myself by trying to close the gap I thought the honest way was to make the gap its own reality, much like memory was not the thing remembered but its own version of the thing. The "everything in" approach I had attributed to Whitman made even more sense now. We do not experience life as a cohesive, linear progression of events and thoughts. Experience comes at us from all angles at different speeds and varying density. Memory on the other hand is selective. Memory is the result of some mental pre-editing. We never again get to see the film's full footage, most of which is left on the cutting floor of history. The task as I saw it then was to create a new reality that was so strong it honored the reality

105

remembered while demonstrating the nature of memory and personal myth-making itself.

I thought one way to bring forward this new reality was to use words in the form of phrases, snatches of memories, anecdotes, family lore and to write them or paint them directly into the paintings. This would add a dimension of understanding that the mere images could not convey by themselves.

****

In art truth is suggested by false means.
                                        - Edgar Degas

****

Patchogue

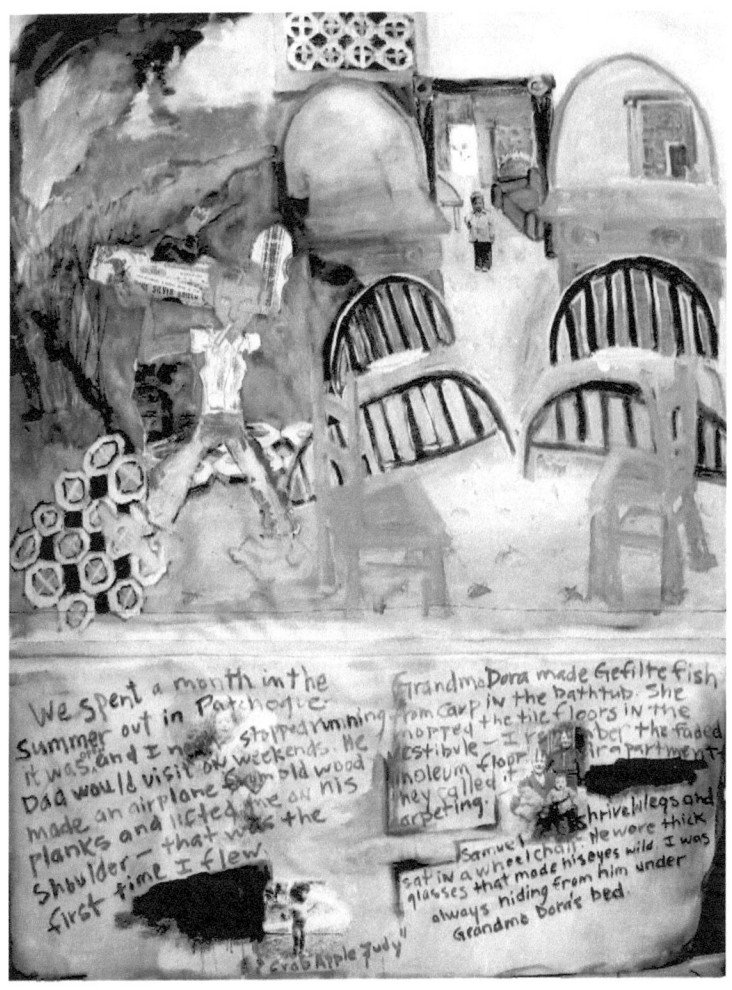

We spent a month in the Summer out in Patchogue. It was, and I never stopped running. Dad would visit on weekends. He made an airplane from old wood planks and lifted me on his shoulder — that was the first time I flew.

Grandma Dora made Gefilte fish from carp in the bathtub. She mopped the tile floors in the vestibule — I remember the faded linoleum floor they called it carpeting.

Samuel sat in a wheelchair. He wore thick glasses that made his eyes wild. I was always hiding from him under Grandma Dora's bed. He had shriveled legs and

"Crab Apple Judy"

My father was a craftsman. I think that is why he became a Certified Public Accountant. He liked the precision of a long column of numbers, the mortise and tenon of a clean balance sheet, the dovetailed solidity of a good profit and loss statement. That is why he loved making furniture as a hobby. Sadly, his life could not be crafted as precisely as a balance sheet or a piece of furniture. Life came at him more like a Jackson Pollack painting and my Dad never did take a liking to modern art.

I remember when he personally built a family room addition to our house in Malverne. He finished it with knotty pine tongue and groove timber and wide planked, pegged floors. He then added built-in cabinets and shelves. I have a picture of him in my mind squinting through his cigarette smoke as he held the level against the wall to be sure the shelves were perfectly straight. I still have a cabinet he made with a tile top. Today it looks a bit primitive, bearing the scars of moving trucks and flights of stairs from Long Island to Massachusetts to Minneapolis and back again to Massachusetts.

I sometimes think art is the relentless pursuit of the ephemeral, an attempt to wrestle with Jacob's elusive angel, gossamer made real. I also think that as in art, so in life. I wonder if this was not my father's windmill, insisting that reality resided in the tangible. And that is why so much eluded him. He expected that if he adhered to a concrete code of decency that things would turn out the way they were supposed to. If you used the plumb line of ethics and principled behavior, the outcome would be the just rewards of a life properly lived within the columns. How he miscalculated. His own body betrayed him and my mother at an all-too-early age. The commute on the Long Island Railroad turned into nightmarish treks of smoke filled delays and breakdowns and always the last minute dash to catch the 5:37 from Penn Station to Malverne. But how could he have fully known all this when we were younger and spent summers in Patchogue, and the green grass and lush trees of Long Island held the promise of a good life, and he taught me how to drive a good straight nail into the wall of our family room.

Dad grew up poor in the Brownsville section of Brooklyn. He used to say most of his friends were either dead or lawyers. In truth, most were businessmen. He was fond of letting his kids know that back in the day the movies cost five cents for two people and, according to him, "I was always on the 2 cents side." He would stand outside the theatre and bark "I've got the two who's got the three?!" He dreamed of making it to the suburbs. He worked since he was 8 years old. Always kicking half of what he made back into the family till. He started City College at night but had to drop out because he couldn't afford the ninety dollars per year tuition. So he ended up going to Pace Institute for two years. He says he always knew he wanted to be a CPA. He was a math whiz and graduated from high school at sixteen. In fact, he never even trusted adding machines. I remember when he had his own accounting firm he would challenge associates to beat him at adding columns of numbers. They would use an adding machine and he had only his pencil to race down multiple columns of numbers and quickly jab the totals at the bottom. He won more times than he lost and sometimes when he lost the associates numbers didn't add up either. When he got out of Pace the state of New York had just passed a statute that required you had to graduate from college in order to take the CPA exam. He managed to be the last person in the state to pass the exam without a college degree.

During the summers, while living on East 33rd, we would spend a month in Patchogue where we rented a bungalow. Dad would drive out on weekends.

Before we moved to Malverne, Patchogue became emblematic of the divide between Brooklyn and Long Island—a vast chasm between old and new ways, tradition and modernity, the wedding halls of Brooklyn and the golf courses of Nassau and Suffolk Counties, the crowded streets of Pitkin or Atlantic Avenues and the endless expanse of Sunrise Highway. To me the gap was traversed by the long drive we regularly took from Malverne to Brooklyn up the Southern State Parkway, the Belt Parkway to Pennsylvania Ave, Linden Blvd to Chester Street where Grandma Dora and Grandpa Meyer lived.

I always felt pressed in by Brooklyn. Brooklyn was filled with strange and threatening characters like Samuel. Samuel parked himself outside Grandma Dora and Grandpa Meyer's apartment. He had shriveled legs and thick glasses and a nearly bald head and he sat in a wheel chair. He was only 16 years old but looked like an old man. He even had thick dark stubble growing on his face. Samuel had it out for me. He always seemed stationed by the front stoop as though he knew exactly when I would be coming outside. He would tell me about the mean men who lived in the buildings on the street and if I wasn't careful they would come and get me—even if I was inside. He once grabbed a pink rubber ball I was playing with and refused to give it back and he threatened to get the mean men after me if I told anyone he had taken the ball from me. I got in the habit of looking out my grandparents' bedroom window to see if Samuel was outside before stepping out. He almost always seemed to be there so I spent hours in their bedroom throwing the ball against the wall and playing catch with myself. The walls were entirely bare with only one exception: a large, old sepia photo of Grandpa Meyer in a Czar's army uniform set in a large oval frame. His shoulders were set back and erect, his head tilted slightly upward. He had the visage of a proud man, his eyes absent of any sense of irony or premonition of things to come. How could he have imagined the journey that would take him to this sparsely furnished apartment in Brooklyn? Simple iron framed beds sat against opposite walls. Grandma Dora made them up with white bedspreads and a single, white clad pillow.

Plain wooden chairs sat next to each bed. At the foot of each bed, against the wall, were two simple chests of drawers, each backstopped with a large oval mirror. On top of Grandpa Meyer's chest of drawers sat a *siddur* and a hair brush. Grandma Dora's chest of drawers had a sheet of glass on top and under the glass were photos of her children and her children's children. It was from her chest of drawers several years later I would steal a $5 dollar bill and use it to purchase a gun and holster set back in Malverne. Alarmed that a seven year old would be toting a saw buck by himself, the shopkeeper alerted my mom. I don't think I had ever seen or would ever again see a look of such disappointment and betrayal as I witnessed on my mother's face. My punishment was to wash Grandma Dora's floors and to apologize and to save my allowance until I had enough to pay the debt back. And of course to forever carry with me the look on my mother's face. Sometimes I think my longing for redemption must date from that experience. I have never been able to get rid of my profound sense of guilt to this day.

One day I found myself in a quandary. I had been bouncing a rubber ball on the front stoop of my grandparent's apartment. The ball rolled down the sidewalk and toward the street curb, but when I turned back toward the stoop after retrieving the ball I found myself staring at Samuel who had come from nowhere and placed himself directly in front of the stoop. I froze in place tingling with fear and foreboding. Something grabbed a hold of me and I began to run. I ran down Chester Street and kept going. I ran under the El and past a group of shops. I just kept running and didn't realize I had dropped the ball somewhere along the way. I remember ducking into an alley between some stores and finding myself staring into the rear of a poultry shop with crates of white feathered chickens madly clucking away. I felt that I was all chest, gasping in deep dry heaves. And then my legs burning. I leaned against the wall and suddenly felt naked, not even having my pink Spaulding ball to comfort me. I stood there for some time. It seemed like a long, long time. The light turned dull, the day fading. A man in a long white apron splattered with blood stepped out of the back door of the shop and pulled a frantic chicken from the crate. The chicken was clucking and flapping and scratching. The man sat down on a bench, folded his elbows over the chicken and yanked its neck. For the briefest moment time and sound froze. The chicken fell limp and the man began plucking the white feathers. I stood there the entire time, forgetting about Samuel, forgetting about my fear, until the chicken had been stripped clean and its pinkish yellowish skin glistened in the fading light.

Brooklyn is a paradox for me. I am pulled to it, drawn by some strange gravitational force made stronger by the years yet repelled and frightened by many of its memories. I do not pretend to understand this mysterious paradox.

At one point I remember wondering how Samuel got to be so mean. I knew older boys on East 33rd Street and they seemed to like playing with me. I remember asking my mom about this and she said Samuel was really not mean inside. But I couldn't understand how you could not be mean on the inside while you were mean on the outside. Later I came to realize that some things are complicated and you had to be older to really understand. A number of years later—I was still pretty young, although I don't remember how young—I learned that Samuel died when he was 18 years old. I remember feeling relieved. Then I was sad and angry at myself. There were still things I didn't understand.

Patchogue meant space and never having to stop running. I loved to take my clothes off and run and run. It seems my parents were always trying to catch me. There was no Samuel in Patchogue and even if there were, there was enough space to run away from him. I didn't have to worry about mean men either since everyone seemed to know each other and were smiling all the time. Patchogue seemed filled with delights. Streams where you could catch tadpoles. Garden snakes that scampered unexpectedly out of the bushes. Cats and dogs that ran freely. Fireflies at night that you could catch and put into a jar with a lid that my dad had punctured with holes to let the air in. It was an entirely different world where there was no bedtime, no need to leave a hall light on, because you fell asleep in someone's lap and magically woke up in your cot in the morning. Of

113

course, not all adventures turned up roses. There's a picture of me with a swollen black eye from when I ran into a swing. And another with huge welted scratches on my forearm from a tabby cat I ran after and which suddenly turned on me. But most of it was dream like. The war had recently ended and we were still on rations. My mom had saved up enough to buy some baking chocolate and she made me a special birthday cake with chocolate frosting even though my birthday was really in May. Everyone stood around on the bungalow porch and admired the cake. I stood on a bench so I could be at the right height when I leaned over to blow out the candles and lost my balance. I tried to twist my body to regain my balance—hands reaching out to me—only to fall bum first into the cake. Still it was too precious not to eat it so we managed to salvage scoops of the crushed remains.

I flew in an airplane for the first time in Patchogue. One weekend my dad nailed together an airplane from several planks found near an old barn. I remember the planks being green. The airplane was large enough for me to sit in the open cockpit and imagine the grass was green clouds. Then my dad lifted me in the airplane onto his shoulder. He began running around, shouting "vroom, vroom" and I was airborne.

The exhilarating experience of such green openness was merely a test drive for what it would be like living on Long Island. Being held aloft in the airplane, cobbled together by my father's own hands, embodied the sense of hopefulness and possibility that awaited our family. I think that's how my younger sister Mimsi (her birth name is Miriam) came into the world. My parents, seduced by the possibilities of Long Island, gave birth to their hope child a full twelve years after I was born. I believe Mimsi's birth was their way of rooting part of their identity in Long Island, staking a claim that this was their home, their destiny, their future. Judy and I had both been born in Brooklyn. Now they could say that after their parents had come from the old world, after their own children were born in Brooklyn where they were still molting the old ways, that they were fully American with a fully American born child drawn into the world at Nassau County Community Hospital on Long Island.

How could they have known that they would both die in that very same hospital before they could see the full flowering of their own children and their children's children?

Things didn't exactly follow the trajectory of promise we thought had been set in motion in Patchogue. After making the move to Long Island, my father had experienced some financial success and began to invest in land in Naples Florida and hotels in Miami with a group of partners. I remember when I was 12 and 13 years old staying at the Cadillac and Sorrento Hotels in Miami on school vacation not quite understanding why the staff was so attentive to us. Family members wanted part of the action. Dad didn't want to involve them, but they kept pleading. So he accepted $5,000 from Uncle Danny and $2,000 from Aunt Faye. Life was good. Dad went from owning an Oldsmobile 88, two tone green, to an Oldsmobile 98, two tone gray. We belonged to a golf club. Then one day he brought me with him to buy a new car—it was a Cadillac dealership. A couple of days later a two tone gray De Ville arrived with its bold fins ready to transport us to places yet undreamed. That car sat in our driveway like a massive symbol of how far my Dad had come from the days in Brownsville when he hawked for the three cents side of a ticket into the movies.

Looking back I see my father behind the wheel, cigarette dangling from his lips, eyes fixed on the road ahead. I felt completely secure, cocooned in a Cadillac, believing my father must have been infused with a sense of unlimited possibilities. I wonder what was in his thoughts. The next deal? Or perhaps a sense of gratitude? Did he believe the trajectory would go on forever or did some sense of unease scratch at the rim of his consciousness?

Then he was embezzled by associates. He was forced to file for bankruptcy. Now without partners he struck out on his own rebuilding his CPA practice. He paid his family members back even though he was officially bankrupt. My mom got ill and then he did too. Among his papers when he died were stock certificates from penny stocks he had invested in. They were worthless. But I couldn't throw them out. I kept them for decades after his death. How better to use them than to cut them up and collage the pieces onto the canvas in the form of an airplane sitting on my dad's shoulder, with me commanding the cockpit in relentless pursuit of the ephemeral, even then.

And then I think of the ways I disappointed my father. The painful choices that led me down an entirely different life path than the one he had envisioned. Perhaps the seed was planted when I was thirteen and read E.L. Voynich's *The Gadfly*. I was swept up by the romantic revolutionary journey of Arthur (my middle name is Arthur) who was betrayed in his native Italy in the 1840s and 50s by his mentor, a priest who had secretly fathered him—so Arthur sailed off to South America to seek his destiny. After years of menial labor during which he was beaten and scarred, and spiritually tested, he returns unrecognizable to Italy where he becomes a revolutionary leader and seeks redemption, truth and justice. How could I resist—a thirteen year old whose identity was clay to such a powerful literary sculptor? I had always had a strong sense of justice, but Arthur's journey, his physical and spiritual transformation called to me like Ulysses' sirens and heightened my sense of destiny.

My father, not withstanding my dreamy sense of revolutionary longing, had understandably practical aspirations for me. I was to major in accounting and go to law school and become a tax attorney. How can two people love each other so much and live in such entirely different internal worlds? This is a mystery to me. Lord knows I tried to be a good son. I wanted to please my father. I began as an accounting major and dutifully sat in on classes that prepared the future leaders of industry by filling them with debits and credits, assets and liabilities, cost accounting principles and a sense that the earth was theirs to inherit. Yet, my soul yearned for so much more. Every morning I experienced a deep emotional unease as I emerged at the West 4th Street Subway stop and walked straight to West 4th Street where I made a left turn, crossed Washington Square Park and entered the School of Commerce. Until that fateful day when I could stand it no longer and told my father I intended to transfer to the school of liberal arts and study history. I could read my father's emotions in his jaw. When he was upset it would tighten and I could see a knot form at the corner of his jaw bone. And so it tightened when I broke the news to him, and with a look of profound disappointment he cut right to the chase.

"And what will you do with a history major?"

"Teach," I responded, not entirely confident even then in my sense of the future.

"Teach? Teachers barely make a living. You think I am going to pay for your college education so you can go out and make half a living?"

The lines were drawn. I moved to a cheap apartment on W. 13th Street and went to work in the Law School library which paid me $34.87 per week plus 8 free tuition credits per semester. I was on my own. But I was free and I remember the sense of excitement and anticipation the first morning after I transferred to Washington Square College, emerging from the subway station and turning left instead of walking straight and then right onto Waverly. I remember watching the familiar figures still making their parallel way to the School of Commerce and not yet quite grasping what it meant to no longer be one of them. I was on a new path even though I had no idea where it would lead.

Then one evening a year and half later at a family dinner my father casually said to me:

"So, I guess you're serious about this liberal arts thing?"

He always had a keen, dry sense of the ways of the world. My father, the man of many numbers but few words, extended his love by the means available to him. It took a lot for him to give up the dream for his only son. There was much said and unsaid in his question. But it was all a form of love.

I think of Giacometti—always drawing, a cigarette dangling from his lips, his eyes squinting at his subject—his frenetic compulsion to capture the fleeting nature of the thing he was drawing.

At various times he blurts out:

"I'll never find a way out."

"Hell is right there."

"It's your whole face."

"This ought to be forbidden as it is among the Jews."

"The most difficult thing to do well is what's most familiar."

"It's abominable."

"It's hopeless."

Even something as solid as flesh and bones eluded his master's hand. Everything was eligible to be drawn. And eluded. On canvas, on a napkin in a cafe, on anything that would hold his marks. The agitated accumulation of lines scratched by his hand, to and fro, never at rest, until a pattern emerges, an evidence of its presence.

Giacometti's incantations had me recall those of my father as they carried him into the ambulance. He wrapped his hand around my wrist and said "It's not good son. It's not good." At the time I thought he meant his condition was not good. Cancer was winning the war. I needed to be prepared for the worst. Those were the last words he spoke. Now I wonder what he meant. What was not good? Was it his condition? His life? Life in general? I have the image of my Dad, cigarette again hanging from his lips, squinting through the film of smoke as it rises before his eyes, trying to make sense of it all, like the master artist Giacometti barking at the elusiveness of his subject. I thought it was in my grasp, son. And then it was gone.

The unseen in the seen. How does the artist bridge this gap? Is the Patchogue panel more unseen than seen? Is *Memory Calls* itself more unseen than seen? If so, then a painting is ultimately a failure less in its technical faults than in the impossibility of the task itself. To fully express oneself in visual form. Or in written form. Or in any form. Any one mode of creative expression bumps up against the ultimate inability to fully convey that which needs conveying.

Why then make the attempt? Why do we even try to leave an imprint when that imprint is inadequate to the full aspiration of the effort?

I believe it is because of consequence—because to not do so is to deny our humanity. It is the attempt that is consequential—not its imperfections. It is the evidence that matters even in its inadequacy. The artist makes the attempt because he or she extends, beyond expectations of a return, the ultimate act of love—to affirm life, to affirm we have lived, to affirm ourselves and our humanity in all its imperfection.

I sometimes think painting is another form of chanting kaddish, the prayer recited after the death of a loved one.

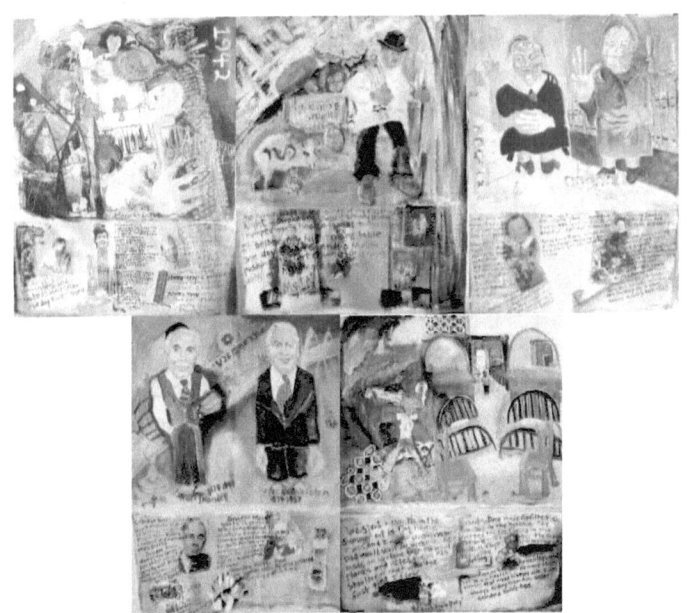

Chiaroscuro

If we begin with the belief that reality is not firm, that it is always changing and that any moment of experience is also in the process simultaneously of becoming and having been—then reality itself is elusive and by extension the accumulation of experiences—as in a life—is also elusive. We can experience our experience in the here and now but only in the here and now. Once experienced our experience is like a puff of smoke unable to be corralled, captured or preserved in any form but in our imperfect memories where, even there, it continuously shape shifts.

We live in the chiaroscuro of life, in the ebb and flow, the emerging and receding, the unfolding and folding and unfolding again. Chiaroscuro comes from the Italian *chiaro* meaning clear, light and oscuro which means obscure, dark. Life is lived in the in-between space, momentarily flickering long enough for us to see, hear, taste, smell, and touch before it continues on its journey to something somewhere else. Our task is to cherish the flickering, embrace the fleeting, love the ephemeral, give gratitude for what we cannot hold onto.

I believe this is what Giacometti and my dad wrestled with. This is what Jacob wrestled with. Call it art, life or angel but really we wrestle with what is impossible to hold onto, with the chiaroscuro, with the mysterious, the illusory. We call these things reality or truth, but really they are but fleeting impressions of things we do not understand, made that much more poignant because we DID experience them. I believe that is the source of melancholy.

And so the artist faces the canvas, the writer/poet the blank page, the composer the empty bar sheet, citizen his/her community and relationships. What is the task? To make tangible and enduring what is believed to have been. To immortalize the melancholy.

How do we know? The illusion of rationality—
we live in a state of chiaroscuro—between the shapes,
between the forms, between the words, the sentences—
neither here nor there—in the unspace space—in
uncertainty, in the question. I sometimes think we are
quarks—unable to be seen truly without a magnifying
lens—in the chiaroscuro we really have no substance—
we only exist in ways the imagination can detect, tickling
out the visible.

A Pleasant Weekend, a True Story

We had just returned from a long walk. The sun
hadn't been visible through the thick morning mist when
we started out. We walked for what seemed miles up the
road and felt the sun burn off the mist and dampness.
Then the sun seemed ready to warm everything up, but a

wind rose and blew the leaves off the branches. In the sun you could watch the glistening leaves glide down onto their shadows.

It was late morning by the time we returned. We would be leaving in just a few hours to head back to Long Island. It had been a pleasant weekend. Not a very long time, but we had to get back to the real world, at least that's what Dad said. Funny how we even discovered the place. Last spring, Mom had been glancing through the New York Times travel section. She spotted old Suits-Us Farm, upstate New York, inviting all the harried suburbanites to a taste of country living. She tucked the ad away and stumbled across it again in the early fall. We hadn't been away together for years. At first, Dad shrugged it off. Business, he said. The next week he changed his mind. Impulse, he said. Dad was never a man of impulse. Judy and I took it as an attempted joke. Nothing more.

Friday afternoon, we had piled into the car. Four hours later we turned into the long dirt driveway of Suits-Us Farm. It was deserted of guests. Harriet and Harold Johnson greeted us so heartily that Dad feared they might embrace him.

"Sure glad to have you people," Harold Johnson said, still shaking Dad's hand.

"You folks were smart coming up about now. It's after the season and you'll have the whole place to yourself. I'm sure you'll like it. Nights are cold, warms up by noon. Plenty of good food. You need anything, we're right at hand," Mrs. Johnson added.

In the morning we bundled into sweatshirts and sweaters and marched off on our first walk. Suits-Us Farm sat at the beginning of a long valley. It wasn't good farming land. The soil was rich enough but the hills were too steep and rocky. The best grazing land nudged alongside the road. Cows lined the road as though it were a trough and munched the grass there. The blacktop road rose and dipped along the bottom ridge of the valley. We followed it with Judy and me leading the way. Mom and Dad fell back by about thirty yards and then around the bend. Two black farm mutts lapped after them but lost interest a hundred yards in and returned to the farm. The dampness held the manure and cut grass smells close to the earth. I breathed it in as deep as it would go.

Judy was excited to get back to the farm to draw. She was in her element and tried to explain to me how there were no lines in nature.

"There really is no such thing as a line. That's only in geometry. In nature nothing is clear cut. There are only colors and shades of color next to each other," she said.

"That must be hard for a beginner to learn," I said.

"Yeah, I'm sure it is. You've got to learn that the pencil and eye are really the same thing. You put on paper only what the eye tells the pencil to. Not what your idea is. Artists create from the shaded areas. In art nature cannot be captured, only implied."

"In nature you can touch a tree," I offered.

"What you touch in nature changes from one moment to the next. Even a tree. That's because of the light." Judy countered.

"You mean artists are not idealists?"

125

"Maybe.   Maybe not. I don't know. I think they're really witnesses."

"It's very sad to be an artist then."

After lunch, I left Judy sitting under a huge maple tree, sketch pad and pencil in hand, drawing Mom and Dad, sitting a few yards off in the sun. I had arranged with Johnson's son to saddle a horse and go riding in the hills. Together we climbed the hill in back of the barn where three horses, a cream Shetland, a bay and a dark brown were nibbling crab apples from low lying branches.

"It's kinda unusual for folks to be coming up this time of year," Johnson's son said. "We really weren't expecting anyone. After the holiday we only get friends from town on occasion."

We followed the path alongside a crumbling stone fence.

Johnson's son saddled the bay and told me there was a good view of the valley from on top of the hill. I cut across the open field and rode beside a ridge that turned into a path.

The path led right to the top. Looking down toward the farm I could see Judy still sitting in the shade of the tree. Mom had a blanket over her legs. It was about three o'clock in the afternoon and the sun already hung low in the sky. Mom and Dad's shadows merged together and stretched out along the ground. The wind had died away and they should have been warm and contented sitting there.

I thought of the movies the family had always taken on trips and around the house with Dad's eight

126

millimeter Kodak. I wished I had brought the camera to Suits-Us Farm, but then thought that certain moments were to be remembered and, perhaps, recorded in other ways. Judy was right about the shaded areas. Those were the ones you had to capture. The camera missed all that, flattened them out, and took your attention away from what you should remember.

Sunday morning we all went for another walk. This time we walked together and went a little slower. We got back late in the morning and had a big lunch. Afterwards, we sat by the tree in the sun not wanting to return to Long Island.

"We were lucky to find this place," Judy said.

"Did you get much drawing done?" Mom asked, her black widow's peak still thick despite the treatment.

"Oh yes. It would be nice if we could come back here sometime."

"Perhaps we will," Mom said.

"We will," Dad chimed in.

"I hope so. It would be nice to come back."

"We will," Dad repeated.

We started home early in the afternoon. We had to beat Sunday traffic.

****

Lightning flashes,
Sparks shower.
In one blink of your eyes
You have missed seeing.
-From a Buddhist Koan

****

Pulling Pages

Certain pages in my sketchbooks grab my attention. I pull them from their spiral binding. They cause me to reflect on what I have been calling creativeness. I have always believed that we have constructed false walls between art and life, one rarefied and for the few, the other for the rest of us struggling to get by and making something of our lives. But in truth they cannot be separated. They make up the ecosystem of the soul in which art and life are sun and earth and our longing is the rain.

I have never been satisfied with the dictionary definition of creativity: Bringing into existence that which did not exist before. This is a simple and true definition in so far as it goes but it stumbles over its own clinical simplicity. It leaves me dry and wanting. There is no passion or messiness in this definition. There is no alchemy. In truth, creativity roils:

Double, double toil and trouble;
Fire burn, and caldron bubble.

128

There is something of mischief and transformation to creativity. It is a witch's brew. There's magic to it. Nor is it singular. It is a profusion.

I have been partial to the definition of beauty--*the quality that gives pleasure to the senses or pleasurably exalts the mind or spirit.* Can you taste the spiciness, breathe in the fragrance, touch the softness, hear the siren's call, see, as William Blake tells us, "the eye altering, alters all."

For me creativity is the energy which grows life in its many forms. Creativity is part beauty, part spirit, affirmation, quest, longing, trouble, mischief, mystery and ultimately transformation—all to serve the expansive impulse of the human spirit.

I believe a core question for us is how do we move from episodic creativity to creativeness—the state or condition of sustained creativity. How do we continuously keep ourselves open to the stupendous possibilities of the world around us? How do we individually and collectively cultivate creativeness?

As I have pulled these pages and reflected on what they may mean I have come to understand that creativeness is based on an orientation toward life. Here are what I believe are the foundational elements to this orientation.

Self Awareness

At some point in our very young lives we become aware that we are separate from everyone and everything around us. We realize: We are no longer an extension of our mother. We are discreet beings. We have autonomy. We are alone. In these first raw moments of self awareness we are introduced to the key elements of creativity—freedom, curiosity, fear and the unknown.

Creativeness relates to our choice of what we do with these moments and the ones which follow. Are we paralyzed by the mere intimation of this awareness? Are we empowered by it? What is our first instinct?

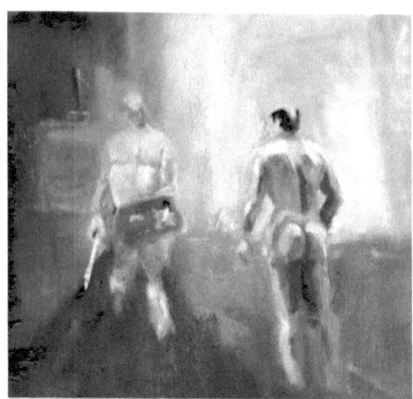

Full Disclosure, Oil

It strikes me that if we wish to experience the full bounty of creativeness, we need to surrender to this paradox of simultaneous freedom and fear. To point the way into unchartered territory. Into the dark wood and shadows of doubt and uncertainty. For every moment we experience both freedom and fear, connectedness and aloneness, is a moment of creative opportunity.

Some years ago Karen and I temporarily moved into a house in close proximity to a church whose bells tolled every hour until midnight. Karen, who has always been a fitful sleeper, found herself unable to nod off in anticipation of the 11 o'clock tolling. Not knowing what to do, she called the church and asked to speak directly to the minister. After listening sympathetically to her

130

dilemma, he said the tolling was not in his hands; however, he tried to comfort her by suggesting she "befriend the bells." The good minister offered wise but unsatisfying advice. Advice that applies to the paradox emerging from our self awareness—simultaneous exhilaration and terror, freedom and aloneness. Befriend the paradox. That's where creativity ripens.

Imperfection

We are told Adam was created with incomplete knowledge and that Eve came from Adam's rib. From the beginning we have been imperfect, flawed. We're damaged goods right out of the box. And the story implies a double whammy for women who are imperfect AND made from the recycled bin of anatomy.

To try to make art is to realize the intractability of our imperfection. We struggle. We aspire, perhaps not for perfection but for something as close as we can get. Is the sublime also too much? We see evidence of a select few nearly touching the stars. Michelangelo came close. Vermeer also. But those are teases. Artists like Goya and Kollwitz more accurately capture our imperfections.

This is why I value those painters who leave evidence of their struggle on the canvas. Painting is not a form of immaculate conception. The final rendition is only part of the story. It is important to appreciate the full process of giving birth, leaving evidence along the way—like Ariadne's string—so we can return and create again. Ariadne, the daughter of King Minos of Crete, had fallen madly in love with Theseus, who was assigned the task of killing the fearsome Minotaur. Ariadne gave

131

Theseus a sword and a ball of red fleece string so he could find his way out of the Minotaur's labrynth

How silly we are to judge ourselves with expectations of perfection, moving us to hide our faults and blemishes as though they are a shameful aberration. We should not fear revealing our bumps and bruises. They are the inevitable inheritance of our nature and deserve to be fully displayed for the truthfulness they represent.

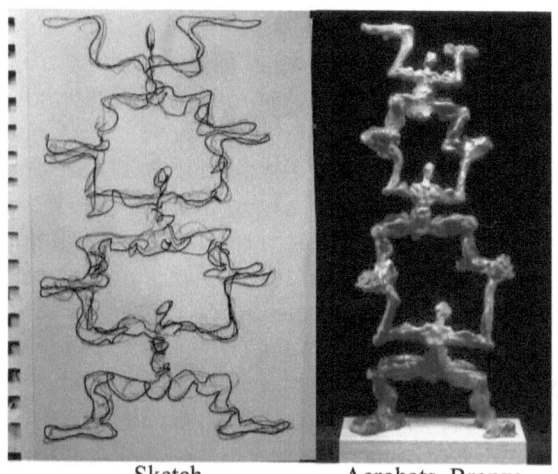

Sketch   Acrobats, Bronze

Vulnerability

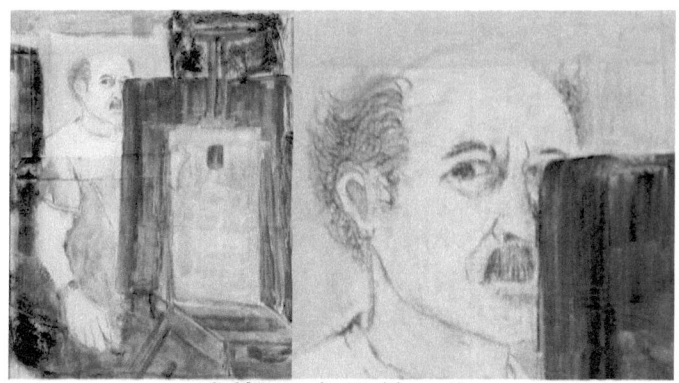

Self Portrait, Multi-media

As artists we must stand naked before ourselves—strip our egos of their garments. The question is: what do we do with the raw, glaring imperfections of our being? Do we make them available for all to see? Do we expose the fullness of our cowardice, our selfishness, our self absorption, our corruptions?

In which one of these two self portraits am I most vulnerable?

Perhaps the question is:

Can I be trusted?

Or perhaps the question is:

Can I trust myself with brutal honesty?

Humility

True artistic expressions must begin in humility because art is less a claim than an inquiry, less a declaration than an exploration, less an ideology than a supplication. Art begins with a kind of self effacement, a kneeling before the mystery of life itself.

Francis Bacon suggests that "the job of the artist is always to deepen the mystery." "You come to nature with all her theories," Renoir tells us, "and she knocks them all flat."

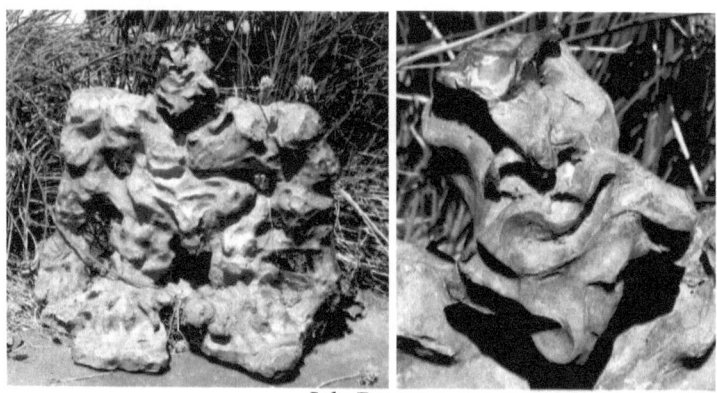

Job, Bronze

Surely, we will end up as Job did before God's awesome questions.

Hast thou entered into the springs of the sea? or hast thou walked in the search of the depth? Where is the way where light dwelleth? and as for darkness, where is the place thereof, Hast thou entered into the treasures of the snow? or hast thou seen the treasures of the hail, Hath the rain a father? or who hath begotten the drops of dew?

Who hath put wisdom in the inward parts? or who hath given understanding to the heart? Canst thou bind the unicorn with his band in the furrow? or will he harrow the valleys after thee?

How do we dare to respond to these questions?

The mystery deepens.

And now we begin.

Empathy

Matisse tells us he does not paint a table. He paints the emotion the table evokes in him. How can one develop his/her creativeness without the capacity for empathy? Art is not an objective endeavor, it is not dispassionate. Artists are not only curious about the world, but feel the world deeply.

In his memoir *Vanished Splendors* the painter Balthus tells us how, in his studio, "I can be satisfied with the progress and advancement of a canvas only if I meditate in front of the unfinished work. With one gesture, I add a single touch. This is slow art, in which the work continues, nonetheless." Wilhem de Kooning, the great Abstract Expressionist, was known to stand in front of an unfinished canvas for hours at a time, silently contemplating what was before him, without making a single brush stroke. And in old, grainy film we can observe Matisse holding a paint brush, circling the canvas again and again with the brush, slowly envisioning the outcome of that magical moment when the brush touches the canvas with its caress.

135

What is going on when Balthus meditates, de Kooning contemplates and Matisse circles? I like to think these are the in-between moments when thought is suspended and empathy fills the heart before the artist leaves an evidence of it on the canvas.

We need more meditation, contemplation, circling in our lives.

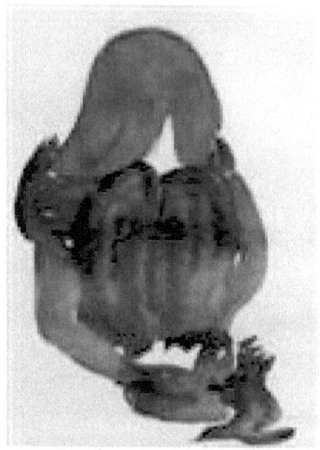

Gardener, Watercolor

Connectedness

In *The Unknown Craftsman; A Japanese Insight into Beauty*, Soetsu Yanagi (1889-1961) master potter writes:

> *A true artist is not one who chooses beauty in order to eliminate ugliness, he is not one who dwells in a world that distinguishes between the beautiful and the ugly, but rather he is one who has entered the realm where strife between the two cannot exist.*

136

This is the truth of Zen Buddhism. Yanagi goes on to tell us that according to a Zen catechism: "Buddha is also dust. Zen monks ask us if the Buddha is not plainly before our eyes in everything."

Everything is Buddha and Buddha is everything. This leads to an underlying connectedness between all things, an orientation toward oneness. Differentiation is an illusion. There are no parts.

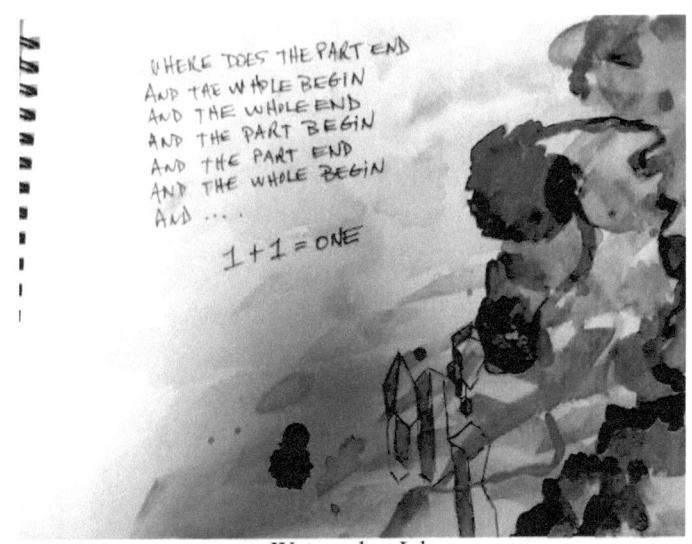

WHERE DOES THE PART END
AND THE WHOLE BEGIN
AND THE WHOLE END
AND THE PART BEGIN
AND THE PART END
AND THE WHOLE BEGIN
AND ....

1 + 1 = ONE

Watercolor, Ink

In Thus Spoke Zarathustra, Friedrich Nietzsche writes:

All that is straight lies. All truth is crooked.

To the western mind all is about complexity and differentiation. The East sees oneness and connection and the West migrates toward categorization and analysis. This leads to a balkanization of experience, a preoccupation with distinctions.

What is an artist living in the world today to do with this dichotomy between complexity and oneness? Is Art also dust? The artist sits at the nexus of a view that embraces oneness as truth and a view that embraces discreteness as truth.

Later Nietzsche says time itself is a circle. Is this an opening? Do East and West meet in the fullness of time and connect back up with each other?

Our consciousness places us on a continuum between connectedness and aloneness. Is this continuum real or illusory? The opportunity for the artist is to capture the interconnectedness of all things, to find a way to express oneness in the profusion, and profusion in the whole. Another paradox? Buddha says paradox is an illusion. Sometimes, I want to believe that.

Longing

Art is our response to our longing for wholeness, connection and meaning. We know we can never realize these fully yet we cannot live fully without them. In some sense we are fated to live in this paradox. That is why we love stories. They provide comfort, even the possibility of redemption. Stories give voice to our longing. Nor can art flower in the absence of longing. Then there would only be beauty or hell. And art grows in the in-between.

Paradox is hands open
Uncertainty trembles
Loosening the grip

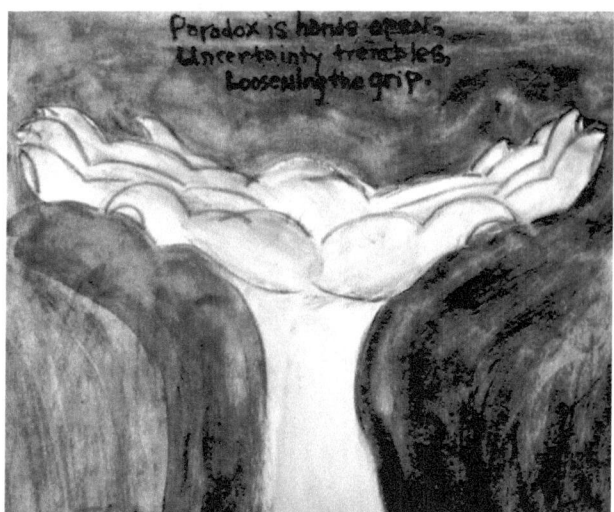

Hands of Paradox, Watercolor, Ink, Charcoal

Multiplicity

We experience life through its particularity. Life throws its cornucopia at us randomly, accidentally, messily. We take it all in through the pores of our consciousness.

When I take a walk in midsummer I sometimes think there are as many variations of the color green as there are stars in the sky. I wonder how many cells make up the human body. How many thoughts come into my head in a given day? I wonder how many stars are in the many galaxies. How many truly? And worlds? And worlds within worlds?

Modern astrophysics tells us that we are made up of the same basic carbon stuff as the sun. In fact, all the other materials in the universe are made of this same carbon stuff. There is a touch of the sun in each of us and therefore we are composed of the common elements of all creation. And yet these common elements manifest themselves in such a phenomenal variety of forms. I wonder how this profusion of forms comes from the same basic stuff. Can the many, in truth, be one?

My grandson Baylor asks me to play Mutant Ninja Turtles with him. I tell him I do not have a sword or nunchuck. He looks at me with a puzzled expression. "But Papi, you can pretend, you can imagine," he encourages me.

Yes, I had forgotten.

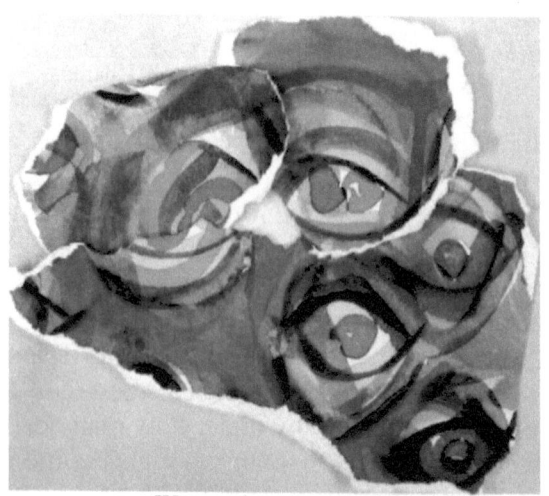

Watercolor, Torn paper

Multiplicity reminds us of the infinite wonders of the universe. Even through the words of a four year old carbon.

Change and Uncertainty

Several years ago I was invited to give a talk to an audience of promising women executives. During a small lunch gathering following the talk one of the attendees described her situation. She was responsible for a major corporate project. She came in early and returned home late. She had two young children and she felt terrible about not seeing them as much as she wanted. At one point she stared over my shoulder as though she were trying to see something in the distance. She said she often felt as though she were at the bottom of a river with the water rushing over her. All she wanted was to get to the other shore, to plant her feet on firm ground and take a rest. She then fixed her eyes on me and asked, "How do I do that?"

I responded: you might not like what I am about to say but in today's world I do not believe there is a shore. It's all river. The question is not how do I get from one shore to the other, but how do I learn to navigate the river so I feel more in control.

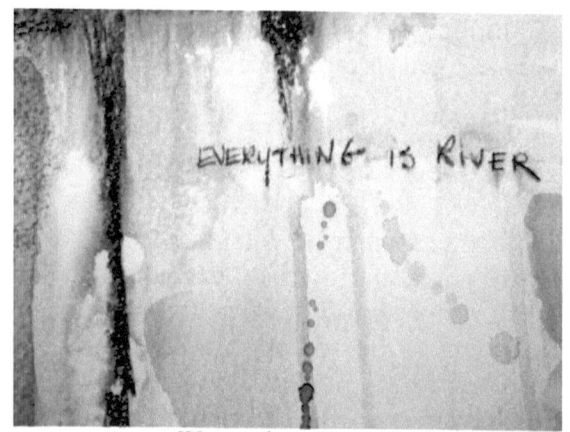
Watercolor, Charcoal

Our lives are a river without shorelines. We live within layers of change, internally and in the external world. If we embrace this reality, then creativeness will be a byproduct.

Love and Hope

Creativeness rises from the soft melancholy of love lost and remembered.

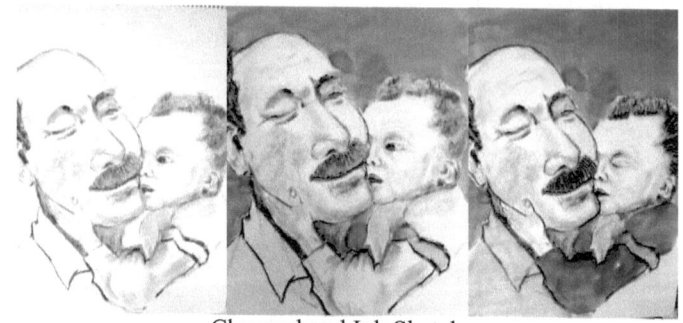
Charcoal and Ink Sketches

At a certain point the thought occurred to me that the artist must love life. But then I caught myself. How can I make such a proclamation when there is so much pain, suffering and injustice? Would the artist love life if he were a victim of such suffering? Would this idealism not become twisted into disillusionment, even rage? And then my thoughts turn to Gautier-Brzeska in the trenches of WWI, Kathe Kollwitz in the midst of the Nazi Holocaust, Francisco Goya during his raging deafness and the Spanish Revolution. And the children of Theresienstadt.

These artists created art through their suffering because they loved life and refused to succumb to despair. Paul Klee tells us "I paint in order not to cry."

Sometimes I weary of the paradox of human goodness and evil. In these moments I believe the artist needs to embrace love because love dissolves all opposites.

Love lays its comforting hand on Thought.

"Rest," Love whispers to Thought, "for just a moment. Allow heart to ascend."

"Rest," Love whispers to Thought, "you will return in your time."

Creativeness comes when Thought heeds the call of Love.

The Poor Man's Way

We live lives of everydayness. We put in place routines that help us manage our lives and allow us to get things done. But the unintended consequence is that we filter out the unusual, the thing worth paying attention to, the outlier, the thing calling for greater appreciation. In my grandson Baylor's world, we filter out BIG. We fear it as distraction, fear it might take us down the rabbit hole of getting nothing done. The result is we file down the edges, shade out the vibrant, blot out the pungent. We live our lives in order to get through the moments, not to truly live them. The purpose of art is to raise the quotidian to heightened awareness and to transmute the everyday into mystery, discovery and reverence. Art is a poor man's way of living a rich life.

Beyond the Studio

Toward the end of working on *Memory Calls* I learned I had skin cancer. The mere word cancer, conveyed in the cold clinical surroundings of the doctor's office, caused an abrupt, discordant pause in the natural rhythms of my life. Fortunately, the particular kind of cancer they discovered—basal cell—is the least aggressive form and after a surgical procedure to remove the intrusive ganglia, I have been sent on my way with the knowledge that I have a fifty percent chance of a recurrence within the next five years.

So I wonder about legacy and the wider world.

I wonder whether *Memory Calls* has meaning beyond the studio and even beyond the work itself. I wonder what the creative process of working on *Memory Calls* reveals about life beyond the studio. Has the project been an exercise in self discovery only? Is creativeness simply a private experience, a deeply personal encounter between the artist and his work? Are there lessons that can be taken into the wider world and serve some larger purpose? Is creativeness as much about how we create our lives and our world as it is about how we create art?

The initial impetus for *Memory Calls* arose from my five weeks in France, my time in Paris, the Bayeux Tapestry, the pilgrimage to the American Cemetery at Omaha Beach and my deep sense of loss. Strangely, the physical distance from my home created the space for thoughts and emotions to bubble to the surface and put me in touch with parts of myself I had only the slightest inkling existed. But the whole creative process of listening to myself in a new way helped me appreciate the powerful interconnectedness between personal experience, history, memory and the world we live in. Each, in its way, contributes to the composition that makes up who I am and who we are. So it is difficult to reflect on and write about *Memory Calls* without making a foray into the world beyond the studio and asking some fundamental questions.

And this brings me back to paradox.

I think of Grandmas Dora and Sarah and Grandpas Meyer and Harry. Immigrants to a strange land. They traveled the road uneasily, never quite understanding or belonging, always having a look of anticipation and uncertainty in their eyes. There was a sense akin to what W.E.B. Dubois called "twoness" related to the Black experience in America—"this sense of always looking at one's self through the eyes of others" causing the individual to question whether he belonged. But the new Jewish immigrant in the birthing years of the twentieth century also deeply felt this sense of "twoness." Language set them apart instead of connecting them to the general culture. Their customs were different. They required a different institutional infrastructure to support these customs. Their Jewishness sat at the very core of their being and emanated outward. It was not a kind of entombed artifact for the general culture to be curious about. They made the journey not to find a home for themselves as much as for their children. Here is where the black experience and Jewish experience diverge. The Jewish immigrants made a choice. They always sat uncomfortably side by side with their truth, simultaneously citizens of and immigrants to their early 20th century adopted land, a part of and apart from, their new world. And yet here I am with an equal but different sense of being a modern immigrant to the 21st century, both in place and time. I too feel like a stranger. Both citizen and immigrant, a part of and a part from this new emerging world.

I have come to realize that *Memory Calls* is not simply a series of paintings or an effort at creativeness, but it is a lens through which I have come to see this wider world. *Memory Calls* is a form of storytelling. It is about how we assemble the snatches of memory and try to organize them into a narrative of meaning. It is about finding oneself in the collective story and understanding how the collective story shapes the individual experience. And it is about how one cannot stop at the studio's edge. The wider world and the studio are interrelated, interdependent, co-creators. An artist may choose to remain only within the studio but he may also choose to step beyond and share his observations, informed by what happens within. Art becomes a penetrating eye through which the wider world is observed and interpreted.

****

The secret awaits for the insight
Of eyes unclouded by longing;
Those who are bound by desire
See only the outward container.
    -Lao Tzu—The Way of Life

****

These words are not to be read,
Rather pondered.
Take them into the woods,
Deeper in.
Hold them to the inquisitive sunlight
Fold them into the entreating shadows
Embrace them by the restless stream
Until they molt their antiquated meaning
And freshly cleave to your soul.

****

What do I see looking at the wider world through the lens of *Memory Calls*?

I see the human endeavor as a form of collective creative expression. We reach into our past for clues of who we are. We arrange and rearrange these clues into what we call history—a tapestry questing for coherence. We stumble through the present perplexed by its many crosscurrents, feeling the stabs of despair yet grasping at hope. We gaze imperfectly into the future trying to discern some silhouette of possibility. And we move inexorably forward before the hands of time tap us on the shoulder. We dance, like marathon two steppers, before the music stops.

I believe we live in perilous times. Not because we lack well intentioned and capable persons in our midst. Nor because we are faced with evil persons whose will to power finds all too ready host bodies in political

147

ideology or religious faith or economic systems. I believe we live in perilous times because we are abdicating the language of art and creativeness to the language of efficacy, growth, productivity, competition.

And when we abdicate the language of art there will be no one to speak for the human spirit. When we stop using words such as beauty, when we glaze over at hearing or seeing Keats' words—"Beauty is truth, truth beauty, that is all ye know on earth, and all ye need to know"—and think them quaint artifacts of a bygone time or judge them overly romantic sentiments then we place ourselves in jeopardy. Not because these words are the ending point of our conversation but the necessary beginning point.

It Will Be Very Beautiful

My heart breaks when I think of the great German artist and lithographer Kathe Kollwitz (1867-1945.) Throughout her life she made courageous choices. She originally aspired to become a painter, but instead chose to work in a less popular and less profitable medium—lithography—because she believed it best captured the subject she wanted to portray—the outcast, the working class and the underprivileged.

In 1891 she married Dr. Karl Kollwitz and moved to the Prenzlauer Berg district of Berlin where Karl established his practice serving the industrial poor. Kollwitz was powerfully drawn to the dignity of these people despite their grinding poverty. Surrounded by child mortality, she undertook an etching in 1903 entitled Woman with Dead Child. As she worked on the etching, she struggled mightily with its emotional and technical demands. She recalled: "When he (her son Peter) was

148

seven years old and I made the etching Woman with Dead Child. I drew myself in the mirror, holding him in my arm. That was very tiring, and I moaned. Then his little child's voice said comfortingly: 'Don't worry Mother, it will be very beautiful."

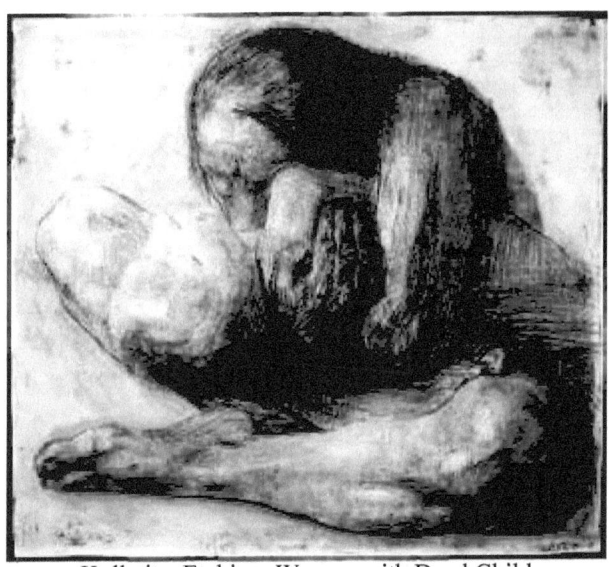

Kollwitz, Etching, Woman with Dead Child

Eleven years later Peter volunteered for service at the outset of WWI and was killed several months later.

How could Kollwitz have known it was the death of her own child she was drawing!!!

I cannot help but ask which voice do we listen to?

To the naïve, hopeful, innocent voice of the child—

"Don't worry, Mother, it will be very beautiful"—
or to the cold, hard world that tries to grind us?

After Peter died Kollwitz confided her grief in her
diary and continued her work. When another German
scourge blighted the world decades later she defied the
Nazi's threats to be thrown into a concentration camp by
refusing to stop creating her "degenerate" art. She
resisted pleas from friends to come to the United States.
She continued to work in her native Berlin. She died in
1945 three weeks before WWII came to a close. Her last
lithograph—from a poem by the German Poet Johann
Wolfgang von Goethe—is titled: *Seed corn must not be
ground.*

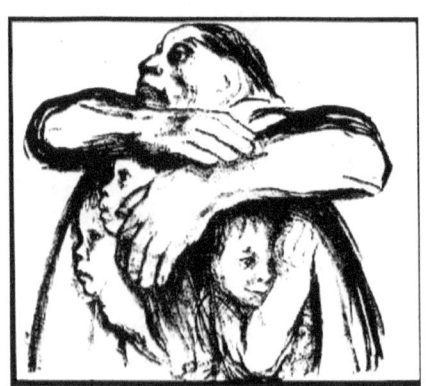

Kollwitz, Charcoal
Seed Corn Must Not Be Ground

Kathe Kollwitz never stopped heeding her son's
"little child's voice."

Homo Imaginor

Practicality and the Will to Power are the enemies of art, creativeness and the human spirit. They work cunningly to bend us to their needs. There is no noble end to power, only an appetite for more of it.

We must not be afraid to speak of beauty. Our governing language, filled with words like growth, productivity and efficiency, is the language of Economic Man. In truth, these terms leave the soul thirsting.

We need to heed the child's voice. And ask the question: what does beauty in the world look like? How can our organizations and institutions contribute to bringing beauty into the world? This is not fashionable. It is not practical. But we need to reclaim our emerging future from the language of those who will bend us toward the practical and the powerful.

Ah, but I can hear Economic Man's laughter: You naïf! Don't you know how the world really works? Without Economics we would be poor indeed. Art is soft. Esoteric. Distracting. Balm to the odd and outliers. This creativeness thing is fine for children at play or the Venice Biennale. But for us, leadership is about getting from here to there and bringing others along. Leadership is tough-minded and results-oriented. We must grow or die.

But here's the rub: the way the world really works according to Economic Man is not the way the human spirit really works.   How do we explain that the materially wealthiest nation on earth is also among the lowest in life satisfaction? Does Economic Man expect to make it up on volume? Besides, Economic Man is missing a key question.   Toward what end do we live and lead? Higher profitability? Greater growth? More efficient production? Toward what end?

Nor are the will to power and the dominating language of economics the only threats to creativeness. Of a lower order but in many cases a more insidious threat is the Practical Person. For such a person Utility is the highest order value. The Practical Person has a built-in sonar that scans for efficacy, efficiency, productivity, serviceability, convenience, appropriateness—the bland array of the tried and true. The Practical Person does not see past his or her current context. For this context is the sum total of the Practical Person's reality. The Practical Person has little patience for dwelling in the imagination, among the outliers—little tolerance for the unknown or ambiguous. The Practical Person is a reductionist and is quick to judge that which cannot pass the litmus test of well worn belts and suspenders. The Practical Person, without malice intended, has a gift for making the Creativeness Person feel that s/he lacks an essential quality of being a contributing member of society.

Of course, we need practicality. We need folks to be able to translate grand and transformational ideas into real stuff and this is the gift of the Practical Person; but the Practical Person is not equipped to lay judgment on transformational ideas because such ideas are by nature impractical. They shift the normal rules the Practical Person is accustomed to applying. So we must teach the Practical Person to suspend what he is most comfortable with for the sake of breaking through to new ways of seeing.

And of course we need economics. We need to clothe and feed ourselves. We need to eliminate poverty. But we do not need to allow our desire to eliminate one kind of poverty to lead to other kinds of impoverishment.

We all know that the Practical Person and Economic Man are utilitarian and therefore they are by all means sober. So let us suggest how art, creativeness and beauty are above all sober and practical and can make leaders better leaders.

Art teaches us how to see. When I use the term art, I mean it in the broadest sense. Not only the visual arts, but music, poetry, dance, theater, crafts, memoir, fiction. Each of these artistic forms teaches us to see in different ways. I know most of us do not consider ourselves artists. But most of us consider ourselves appreciators of at least one art form or another. For both the practitioner and the appreciator, a critical truth is that embedded in the art-making process are core capabilities that equip us to live and lead creatively and with impact in our modern world. Observing the world through the art making process challenges our conventional view and can open unexpected possibilities.

I believe every adult should take a drawing class. I know the immediate response by most people to such an idea would be: are you kidding!? And embarrass myself! No way!

I am serious. Drawing changed my life by changing my perspective.

I enrolled in my first drawing class at age 55. Although I had been doing sculpture for a few years I had not taken an actual drawing class since the 7th grade. Sculpture did not require drawing so I was your typical, everyday stick figure drawer.

When I entered the classroom for the first time I was self conscious. I felt truly naked. And my teacher did not make it easier.

At the first session, I stood at an easel with charcoal in hand. Fifteen feet away sat a live female model. I began to work, trying to draw the contours of her figure. As my instructor moved from student to student he paused in front of each easel and commented on the student's work. When he came to me he glanced at the work and moved on without comment. During the second class I found myself flushed with nervousness as he made his rounds. My anxiety spiked as he approached my easel. Would he stop? Would he comment? And what would he say? Or would he just keep going as he did in the first class, leaving me in a state of sweaty suspense?

Only this time he did stop. He stroked his beard and then turned his palms up and asked: "What are you doing?"

He didn't ask what are you trying to do? Or what would you like to do? It was: What are you doing— clearly indicating I had a total lack of even a rudimentary understanding.

As a mature adult I found myself stammering: "I'm looking at the model and I'm just trying to render what I see."

His response shot from his lips. "No, no, no! You do not see in order to draw, you draw in order to see."

He repeated the refrain for emphasis. And then he moved on.

I felt as though I had not taken a breath in several minutes. After letting out a fully audible sigh, I realized I had just been the recipient of a revolutionary readjustment, a radical reframing of the very nature of drawing.

I also felt suddenly and remarkably free.

Drawing was not about seeing something and trying to copy it. Drawing was a process of discovery—you draw in order to see! You draw in order to discover the nature of the thing you are trying to visually describe. Since drawing was less about precision and replication, I realized, then I was suddenly free to explore with my eye, hand and charcoal all kinds of relationship. My hand became looser, my charcoal strokes more expressive. My sense of excitement and anticipation grew. I was an explorer of new terrains. A mass here, a darkening there, a form fading there. I was talking to myself and to my hand. I was working more rapidly, less deliberately. I was SEEING things and relationships I hadn't noticed before. And what emerged on the paper was something quite remarkable, filled with boldness, energy and originality. I stood in awe at what was in front of me on the easel, not because it was exceptional by any measure but because it had come from a place within me that I did not know was there.

We each have in us this something that we do not know is there.

The process of drawing, of making art is the process of learning to see in new ways. By adopting an art-making mindset we hone the skill of making sense of the world in ways that conventional thinking cannot reach.

Art teaches us how to suspend our preconceptions, our habitual approaches and enables us find new relationships, new discoveries. What emerges when we look in this way is always surprising and remarkable.

When Rembrandt teaches us to see the inner person in his portraits, when da Vinci teaches us how meaning lies in the in-between space between things, when Monet teaches us to see the shifting nature of light, when Picasso and Braque show us through Cubism how different perspectives add up to a whole, when Cezanne teaches us the beauty of geometry and harmony in the world, when all these artists teach us how to see in different ways, they are not only teaching us about art. They are teaching us that the practiced eye can see through and around current realities and challenges to new possibilities, solutions and innovations.

In the introduction to *But Is It Art?* the brilliant physicist Richard Feynman wrote: "I wanted very much to learn to draw, for a reason that I kept to myself: I wanted to convey an emotion I have about the beauty of the world."

It is no accident that one of the most important physicists of his generation turned to art to understand and convey an aspect of experience that he could not access through science or, in fact, in any other way. He saw the kinship between science and art—to convey "a feeling of awe" about "the glories of the universe."

Feynman is telling us why we must adopt an artist's mind set. Monet tells us how: "It's on the strength of observation and reflection that one finds a way," Monet tells us. "So we must dig and delve unceasingly."

It is this very ability to access insight through the arts that makes them so essential to leaders.

Art embraces uncertainty. We live in a sfumato world. Sfumato means "up in smoke." And it refers to a painting technique utilized by Leonardo da Vinci in the Mona Lisa which creates the sense of fuzziness or smokiness in a painting. It is not only the expression on Mona Lisa's lips that is shrouded in ambiguity and

156

uncertainty. If we look carefully at the landscape in back of Mona Lisa we see the smoked haziness of the trees and rivers. It is hard to delineate where a tree ends and the rest of the landscape begins. Da Vinci is telling us there is uncertainty not only in us but around us. Our world is filled with sfumato, with smokiness, fuzziness. It is often unclear where a problem ends and a solution begins. We put our heads down on a pillow at night in a world that is very different than the one in which we awoke hours earlier. Change is constant, rapid and then it begins all over again. Only faster.

A complex, rapidly changing and disruptive world requires a different set of skills, sensibilities and orientation. Eric Schmidt, former Chairman and CEO of Google, gives us a practical sense of how this uncertainty plays out in the real world. "… great ideas often emerge. You can't get to them by taking the most direct route because you don't know the destination in advance. You think you're working on one thing, but the really important thing turns out to be something else entirely, something on the periphery of what you thought was important. I've seen this happen again and again."

Yet, in order for great ideas to emerge, we need to learn the openness that art offers. We need to ride the waves of uncertainty with equanimity and alertness, with patience and mindfulness, qualities which invite emergence. The great poet John Keats called this Negative Capability. Great work emerges, he tells us, "when man is capable of being in uncertainties, mysteries, doubts, without any irritable reaching after fact & reason…." In other words, let the divergent, the exploratory, the suspension of belief and assumptions have their day. Do not move toward convergence or resolution too quickly.

157

But for many of us, even most of us, our impulse leans toward paralysis or pushes toward resolution. If the world is not knowable, if things are always shifting, if we are confronted by complexity upon complexity, then the task may appear impossible. Art does not accept impossible. Rather it advocates the generous, expansive embrace of the world as source and inspiration by developing our mindfulness, tuned into the ripeness of what is observed, even if what is observed seems uncertain or opaque. Art invites us to embrace this uncertainty as a source of new possibilities.

Art teaches us how to disrupt before we are disrupted. Art teaches us to invite disruption as part of the normal process of creating and recreating. In many ways art is the intentional introduction of disruption as a precondition for creativity and innovation, for re-imagining a different world. Picasso suggests that every act of creation is first an act of destruction. Art demonstrates that disruption is not to be feared.

I have been teaching a program entitled "The Leader as Artist" at MIT Sloan School of Management to MBA students and Advanced Fellows. None of the participants have an art background. They come from all over the world with a wide range of work experiences. For one exercise I construct an impromptu pile of chairs into a tangled sculpture of flat plains and lines and jagged corners. On top of the sculpture I place an apple.

I then ask the students to draw what they see on a large sheet of paper using charcoal sticks. They take the exercise seriously and you can see the intense concentration in their eyes. Over several minutes of focused work they become deeply engaged in their drawing. When I ask them to show their drawing to their classmates you can see their sense of accomplishment. I then instruct them to tear the drawing into at least four random pieces.

Gasps of resistance fill the room. The air goes out of their bodies. Their smiles turn to furrowed brows. One or two of the participants blurt out "No! No way!"

I then ask them to choose any two sections of their torn work and to glue it to a fresh, clean sheet of paper. I invite them to move to a different position in the room and to draw the sculpture again. I suggest they find a way to incorporate the residual pieces they had glued onto the paper into the new drawing. They can draw around, over, through their previous marks.

Again they throw themselves into the task. Only now they appear a bit more tentative, as though the prospect of another imminent disruption is tempering their full engagement with the drawing. At the end I have them hold up their new drawing for display and they reluctantly acknowledge the product of their efforts has a depth and richness that the first rendering lacked. Nonetheless some of the students indicate they expect me to have them tear up this new piece of work as well. Instead we moved on to another topic.

Later in the session we return to their drawings. They immediately understand their task even though I have not yet given them any instructions. So they tear their latest drawing into several pieces and paste a few of the torn scraps onto a new sheet. Only this time, some participants glue pieces so that they hang over the edge of the paper. In a few cases they paste pieces over each other rather than as separate pieces. In one case a participant glues scraps on the fresh sheet of paper and folds that in half and glues the two halves together so the surface becomes bumpy from the underlying pasted pieces. Another participant pulls a theatre stub from his pocket and pastes it into his drawing. I have not instructed them to do any of this. Their actions come spontaneously and of their own making and, I must add, with a sense of renewed energy and anticipation.

As we discuss the experience and deconstruct the process, the students gain a wide range of insights. Disruption is intensely unsettling the first time. It is unsettling the second time. We get over invested in the product of our efforts, they suggest. We experience negative emotions. These negative emotions get in the way of fully tapping into our creativity. By the third time the disruption is seen as an opportunity to re-engage, refresh, reinvent. Confidence grows with each disruption. The product of each disruption is deeper, richer, and more inventive than each of the previous disruptions.

Responding to disruption is a skill that gets stronger with practice.

We have been told disruption is the enemy. In truth, disruption unsettles and deepens. Disruption provokes and enriches. Disruption is the gateway to renewal and innovation. We must learn to proactively disrupt with intention, not with fear.

Art empowers imagination. The Dutch historian Johan Huizinga (1872-1945) questioned the accuracy of the term homo sapiens. Living through the Nazi occupation and interred in a holding camp, he wryly observed that "we are not so reasonable after all...." Huizinga preferred to refer to mankind as *Homo Ludens*, Man the Player, or *Homo Faber*, Man the Maker. But I would suggest still another descriptor, one which is the fundamental differentiator of the human species. We only need to visit the caves at Lascaux or Chavet in France or Altimira in Spain. It's right there on the cave walls—30,000 to 40,000 years ago.

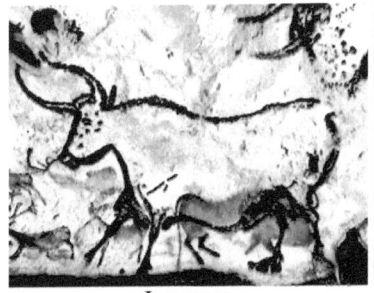 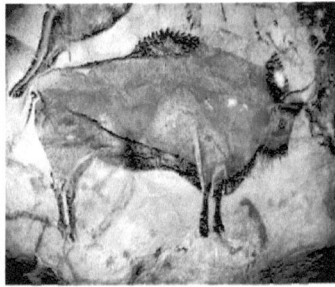

Lascaux   Altimira

Concurrent with wondering where their next meal would come from or whether they might be swallowed up by a saber tooth lion at any moment, these cave dwellers were scratching images from pigments and animal fat. Iron oxide was used to paint in red, manganese oxide for black and ochre provided yellow hues. (One could even argue that art is the mother of chemistry!)

Before we are knower, maker or player we are *Homo Imaginor*. In Latin, *imaginor* means the ability to envision or create something in one's mind.

To create art is as fundamental as the drive to meet our basic physiological and safety needs. As my four year old grandson Baylor so often reminds me, our capacity to imagine makes knowing, making and playing possible. Before we can change the world we need to imagine a different one.

In his maverick-spirited book *Orbiting the Giant Hairball: A Corporate Fool's Guide to Surviving with Grace*, Gordon MacKenzie tells the story of his visit to an elementary school. He asks a class of first graders

161

how many of them consider themselves artists, and a vast majority of hands shoot up! He then goes into a second grade class and asks the same question. Slightly less than half the hands are raised. And then he enters a third grade class with the same question and only a few hands find their way above the students' shoulders.

What happens to these children between the first and third grades? Whatever it is we are all at risk of becoming those third graders. Becoming fully acculturated and conditioned to no longer think of ourselves boldly, taking risks, unencumbered by the prospects of searing judgments of oddness and impracticality.

We have developed a world view centered on Economic Man based on the underlying assumption that by striving for ever increasing economic and material wealth we will fulfill our highest and best potential. This view is couched in the pseudo-language of rationality, metrics and widgets. As though by virtue of referring to ourselves as homo sapiens, our power to reason, wrapped in an economic solution, will catapult us toward a bright, shining future.

Leaders need art in their lives. Not occasional art. Not an intermittent trip to a museum or gallery. Leaders need art at the center of their lives. They need to encounter the paradigm-shifting power of art. They need to talk to art and have art talk to them. Because art is the voice of the human spirit. It is the language of imagination made manifest. It is the joy of discovery and wonder in the eyes of first graders.

Leaders need to embrace the quest of art: "Art is creative for the sake of realization, not for amusement: for transfiguration, not for the sake of play. It is the quest of our self that drives us along the eternal and never

162

ending journey we must all make." This is the great German painter Max Beckmann's plea.

Any quest begins with a question. *Memory Calls* compels me to believe we need to ask different questions of our wider world.

What do we want beauty to look like in the world?

What would a masterpiece world look like?

How do we create this masterpiece?

What are the tools and skills we need?

How do we develop these tools and skills?

What role can our organizations play in creating this beauty/masterpiece?

How do we enroll others?

Some may say we are too late. We cannot change. The system is too entrenched—it will not or cannot yield. The mercantile paradigm which gave birth to unfettered free market capitalism has been our dominant framework since the 14th century. And this paradigm has locked in a value chain and entrenched interests with no room for such new language.

But we are at an inflection point. I believe there are leaders with the spirit of art and beauty in them. They seek ways to release the full power of their creativeness and that of those they lead. They want to bring these new questions into the public discourse. They seek ways to let the voice in and to amplify it in their lives and leadership.

Art again provides an example of hope.

At the close of World War I, Prime Minister George Clemenceau of France approached his old friend Claude Monet with a proposal. At this point in his life Monet was secure in his international reputation as the father of Impressionism. Clemenceau offered Monet a commission to paint a series of his water lily paintings for the French Nation as a symbol of peace. Clemenceau indicated that they had already reserved several rooms in the *Musee de l'Orangerie* for the paintings. But Monet expressed reluctance to accept the commission. He had turned eighty and his eyes were going bad—he had had several cataract operations. Clemenceau nonetheless persisted and Monet finally agreed.

Despite his age, poor eyesight and declining physical condition, Monet embarked on the project not as a way to repeat his prior water lily paintings but as a way to re-invent them. The water lily paintings that hang in *Musee de l'Orangerie* today represent a work of transcendent beauty. They draw on all the earlier water lily paintings but in an entirely re-imagined form. From layer upon layer of paint emerges the subtle presence of the water lilies, resplendent in shimmering colors, each one distinct, vibrating with its individual energy, yet connected to the roots reaching below the water's surface into an all embracing union of nature.

The viewer has the sense that he is freely and intimately floating among the water lilies. A deep silence descends on all those who enter the space of these paintings. The viewer finds himself simultaneously profoundly alone and powerfully connected to a larger presence. The viewer cannot help but pause and reflect on his place in the magical wonder of nature.

Monet tells us we can change, even at an advanced age.

I can hear the whispered voice of Michelangelo through the ages. He is saying the danger is not that we aim too high and miss but that we aim too low and reach it. Monet and Michelangelo provide a pathway. They challenge us to re-imagine boldly, to lean into possibility, to speak beauty to power, to take risks toward greatness.

Too See A World

But how do we do this? Most of us are not artists. We cannot paint resplendent canvases.

But wait a moment. That is a Practical Person's perspective. It is a perspective whose premise is designed to allow others to maintain control. It is a point of view whose assumptions we cannot accept because, in truth, we ARE all artists. We each may use a different canvas and different medium, but we are artists nonetheless.

William Blake lays the challenge before all us artists:

> *To see a world in a grain of sand,*
> *And a heaven in a wild flower,*
> *Hold infinity in the palm of your hand,*
> *And eternity in an hour.*

What if the whole world were our canvas? What if we reflected on the possibility that our individual thoughts and actions impact the entire world? Would our sense of accountability change? What if our efforts to re-imagine our role as a leader actually effected not only our organization but the entire world? What if we could see the world in the grain of our organization, and new possibilities in the flower of our people, hold the future in the palm of our hands, and eternity in an hour?

I believe the first step is for each of us to step back from the canvas of our day to day lives and to reflect deeply on the possibilities opened by these questions.

And then to reconnect with the power of art and memory to unlock new ways of seeing the world.

I have come to realize that the process of creating *Memory Calls* has led me to a very different place than the one I thought I was moving toward. In the beginning, *Memory Calls* was about remembering and preserving events and people from my past in order to better understand myself in the present. I thought the past was about the past and remembered events were about remembered events. I now realize that this has been a wrong assumption. I am reminded of Kafka's poignant refrain: "I am a memory come alive." Memory is not about the past. Memory tingles in every fiber of the present. The act of remembering is about connecting us to what is most alive in our memories and how this aliveness and the truths within it serve us in the present and become the basis for creating our future. Paradoxically, the remembered past is really about the future. But without remembering what is most alive in our memories we cannot create a future of meaning and fulfillment.

I think of Grandpa Meyer who disappeared for days at a time. No one ever knew where he went. He never told us. I sometimes think it is less important to know where he went than to understand what he was seeking.

I think of Grandpa Meyer bursting in from the snow storm's fury on the Iowa prairie to light a fire on *Shabbos* (despite the rabbinic prohibition against it) and saving Grandma Dora and their young children because saving a life is more important than adhering to the Law.

I think of Grandpa Meyer railing against the thugs who mugged him and stole the watch his children had given him for his 75th birthday. Fist in the air, unbowed, *"Mein kind! Mein kind!"* "My children! My children!" The thieves had not stolen his watch. In his mind they had stolen his children. But they would never understand. He spoke an entirely different language. Not because he screamed in Yiddish but because he shouted about love lost, love stolen, his children. It was not the material watch that mattered to him. It was the meaning of the gift. *Memory Calls* is about the gift we give to each other in the language of love, beauty, and redemption. And the need to pay these forward.

I often wonder what free men and women in a truly free market would freely choose. Would they choose money, productivity, share holder value, efficiency, or would they choose to contribute to a world reaching for its highest potential? And then, again, I wonder about the child in us and whether the impulse to pretend is an effort to escape or the gift of reimagining new possibilities. Four year old grandson Baylor always reminds me that when a situation seems intractable, when you are in danger of tipping toward despair, when you think you do not have what it takes—then imagine—"But Papi, you can imagine," he implores me. He is reminding me that the human imagination is our most powerful tool.

167

It guides us from here to there. It is up to our impulse toward creativeness that takes us the rest of the way.

Our world is torn. In order to repair it we need to promote the ascendency of Homo Imaginor in ourselves, our communities and our world.

While working on *Memory Calls* I read *Matisse the Master; A Life of Henri Matisse*, a wonderful biography by Hilary Spurling. Spurling quotes Matisse in a letter to his daughter, explaining what set him apart from the contemporary sculptor Maillol: "What harmed Maillol a good deal as a sculptor is that he so often called a halt as soon as his work reached a satisfactory stage. And what has helped me a lot is pushing on beyond that point, in spite of the high risk."

Great art, creativeness and the pursuit of beauty require courage, a willingness to step into the unknown. All leaders, in fact all of us, have the opportunity to adopt this Matissean Vow—to not stop at a satisfactory stage—but to push beyond the good enough of current thinking and the language of Economic Man or the wary gaze of the Practical Person.

Memory Calls brought me to the realities of creativeness, paradox and beauty. Memory itself brought me back to what endures in the human spirit. And to our fundamental capacity for imagination. And the power of art to change us. And the possibility of a mended world.

www.ingramcontent.com/pod-product-compliance
Lightning Source LLC
Chambersburg PA
CBHW020910180526
45163CB00007B/2688